WHY YOU SHOULD CLIMB A MOUNTAIN

AND 58 OTHER LESSONS ON HAPPINESS, SUCCESS, AND FINDING YOUR PURPOSE IN LIFE

by

ALON SHABO

For my #1 fan, my mother.

CONTENTS

Section I: Happiness

Section II: Confidence

Section III: Purpose

Section IV: Success

WHY YOU SHOULD CLIMB
A MOUNTAIN

A NOTE FROM THE AUTHOR

If this book triggers just one idea that helps you improve your life…

…something that makes you happier and more confident on a daily basis…

…something that helps you accomplish any one of your goals…

….something that helps you overcome something you're struggling with…

…or something that simply reminds you that every little thing is gonna be alright….

Then I will consider this a great success.

Alon Shabo, March 2017

(aka Richard Arthur)

HOW TO USE THIS BOOK

Each lesson can be read on its own. Skim the table of contents and jump to the lesson that calls out to you right now.

Some people will prefer to use this book as a pick-me-up and read 1 or 2 lessons each morning with coffee.

Others will prefer to read it cover to cover in one sitting.

The choice is yours.

Only you know what's truly best for you.

"Your days are your life in miniature. As you live your hours, so you create your years. As you live your days, so you craft your life. What you do today is actually creating your future. The words you speak, the thoughts you think, the food you eat, and the actions you take are defining your destiny -- shaping who you are becoming and what your life will stand for. Small choices lead to giant consequences -- over time. There's no such thing as an unimportant day."

- Robin Sharma

SECTION I: HAPPINESS

WHAT'S YOUR STORY?

WITH EVERY PASSING second, we are writing our own stories. And the stories we tell ourselves are responsible for most of our results in life.

Your inner dialogue and the stories you tell yourself all dictate what kind of life you live.

Do any of these stories sound familiar?

I don't have the time…

I'm not good enough (or smart or good looking)…

That would never happen…

I don't deserve that kind of happiness..

I am a flawed person.

I don't deserve this.

These are made up stories that directly impact the results we get in life, love, and happiness.

This is destructive wiring that can stem back to a single event in our lives – most of us are aware of these thoughts in our head, yet we're oblivious to the catastrophic implications they have on how we show up in the world.

This flawed "inner game" is what prevents us from making necessary changes in life.

Our inner game sabotages us.

It keeps us in the comfort zone.

The thing is: staying within comfort zones is truly the most horrendous way to decay.

The more challenge and friction you put yourself through – the better your character develops.

You become the best version of yourself through overcoming obstacles, never through ease.

We are writing our own story with each thought we think.

The way we spend our hours are the way we spend our days. And the way we spend our days are how we spend our lives.

Your life is a movie, make it spectacular.

CLEAN OUT YOUR BAG OF SHIT

THERE ARE TWO types of shit bags we all carry around.

The first is the belief that you're not good enough.

And the second is the belief that others are not good enough for you.

Both of these bags of shit hinder your quality of life, confidence, and hurt your relationships.

Your belief system and that inner dialogue is controlled by your inner game – and by nature, it's extremely negative. It's literally the frame in which you view the world around you.

If you're not hip to this, it will subconsciously sabotage your life.

Sometimes it can be traced to a single event in your childhood.

Other times, it's a bit more complicated, and it takes serious work to uncover it.

For some it's a father who was never supportive.

For others, a single event which left you feeling weak and humiliated.

Whatever your bag of shit is, the truth is this.

You've brainwashed yourself.

Your parents and other important figures screwed you up.

You grew up with other people's beliefs, expectations, flaws, and methods.

And because you grew up with all of this, you may have thought it was completely normal at the time.

But it wasn't.

So this shit is literally wired into your brain.

And unless you actively recognize this and actively intervene, these brain connections will get stronger each year. They will become part of your personality.

The solution is to "*let go*" and "*be present*."

You let go of the past lies you invested in and the internalized parent who is always judging you and others.

And you'll find that the world is better, brighter, and easier to navigate than it used to seem.

But all of that is easier said than done, of course.

SELF-IMPROVEMENT IS NOT A DESTINATION

IF YOU VIEW it like that, you'll end up searching more than doing.

Looking more than living.

Can you relate?

You read more and more articles, books, and "life hacks."

You go deeper into the rabbit hole — you need to master X before you can be Y.

You get addicted.

It's numbing almost, this "self-help" stuff. You end up studying self-improvement more than you actually end up improving.

That's not what this is about.

At all.

Self-improvement is about living life as your best self — no matter where you are in your journey.

It's about enjoying this beautiful mysterious thing that is life at the highest level possible.

And to do that, you need to take a step back, be present, celebrate your accomplishments, and focus on what the Japanese call Kaizen — 1% tiny improvements every day (this concept changed my life ... more on that later).

This book is meant to help you celebrate your life as your best self no matter where you are in your personal development journey.

The next few lessons will be all about living life happily and successfully.

We'll be going over things like meditation, exercise, being present, winning morning routines, and way more. These lessons will be about small daily actions that yield large improvements in your quality of life and things you can implement ASAP.

And the best part is that you'll feel the benefits instantly.

PULL YOUR SHOULDERS BACK

THE NEXT TIME you're feeling sad, lethargic, or out of it - pay attention to your posture.

According to cognitive scientists, if you're feeling funky, you'll most likely be slumped over with your neck and shoulders curved forward with your head looking down.

While it's true that you're sitting this way because you feel sad or weak, it's also true that you're feeling sad or weak because of this posture.

Our mind influences the way our body reacts, and the form of our body also triggers our mind.

It's why I'm so big on health, fitness, and awesome habits.

One thing I do before every important call or meeting is a power pose.

Just two minutes of power posing a day can change how you feel.

11

This isn't just about appearing larger, but it actually changes our hormones.

Power poses are proven to increase our testosterone, the success hormone, and decrease cortisol, the stress hormone.

A 2009 study on 71 college students had some interesting takeaways.

The students in an upright proper position felt and associated "empowering and positive" traits about themselves.

While those in the slouched over position were recalling "hopeless, helpless, powerless, and negative" feelings.

The study found that sitting in a slouched over "helpless" position made it easier for negative thoughts and memories to appear, while sitting in an upright powerful position made it easier to have empowering thoughts and memories.

The major takeaway from the study: emotions and thoughts affect our posture and energy levels, and conversely, posture and energy affect our emotions and thoughts.

KILL THE INNER CRITIC

IT'S NO SECRET that you are your harshest critic.

That internal voice is constantly criticizing every move you make.

You're never good enough.

And you can always do better.

Does that sound familiar?

It's totally normal.

As humans in today's over-stimulated world, our brains are wired to be constantly dwelling, obsessing, and stressing about little things that don't really matter at all.

It's too easy to get caught up in the chaotic brain trap, and it's why I stress brain care so much in this book.

In my life, the pivotal moment when things started going

my way and I felt I was finally "on the path" happened when I started prioritizing daily brain care.

Now, this isn't another lesson about exercise, journaling, meditation, or sleeping.

You're about to learn all of that, and more.

This lesson is to serve as your daily reminder.

Loving life pretty much comes down to these two big ideas:

1. Learning to see the beauty in everyday ordinary things

2. Expressing major gratitude, every day.

Notice how there's nothing material or superficial there?

Here are a few ways to put this all into action:

List The Things You Are Grateful For

Gratitude is like a muscle, and it needs to be trained often. Every night before I go to sleep I make a list of the things I'm grateful for.

This always opens my eyes to how good I have it, especially on those days when I feel like my life is a mess.

Do a Monthly and Quarterly Review

At the end of each month, summarize what defined that month.

Was it learning? Struggle? Adventure? Overcoming obstacles?

Wrap up what you did, the big things that happened, what you would do differently, and what you learned.

And every quarter, review your life in the same way a corporation would.

Track things, set goals for the following quarter, and strive to reach them.

Remember, what gets measured, gets managed.

Meditate Daily

I've written about the benefits of meditation time and time again, and I don't plan to stop anytime soon.

Meditate every morning to calm your brain down, get clarity and insight into your thought process, and really just feel happier and more fulfilled altogether.

You can get started with a free app called HeadSpace.

And just remember...

Be present, surrender to the moment, and know that everything in life will always work out for the best.

Everything that happens to you is just a lesson you needed to learn to move forward.

YOUR BRAIN IS A LIAR

OUR BRAINS NATURALLY gravitate towards the stormy side.

Our perspective is biased towards the negative.

Bad is more powerful than good.

The brain favors negativity so much that it skews our vision of reality.

And while most people have 3-4x more positive experiences than negative ones, the brain clings to the negative and hopes to prevent it from happening again.

This is similar to risk aversion, which keeps people indecisive and stuck for life, but today's lesson is different.

Today's lesson is about how the brain naturally hurts our confidence.

And how, without being conscious of this fact, we can be

carrying around "big bags of shit" that wear us down, sometimes for our entire lives.

In our everyday life, we fixate on what went wrong instead of everything that goes right.

And instead of loving our flaws and knowing that they're what make us uniquely human, we obsess about the slightest imperfections — too much this, or not enough of that.

The brain focuses on the negative to protect us. And while it's only trying to keep us alive, it can really hurt our confidence and inner dialogue.

So what do we do about it?

Simply knowing that your brain tends to favor the negative is the first step.

When you catch yourself focusing on all the possible negative outcomes, or dwelling on a past situation, regardless of how realistic they are...

STOP.

This has nothing to do with you; it's your brain.

And it's perfectly normally to get caught up in "negative thinking." But you must stop, realize this, and keep moving forward, in spite of your negative thoughts.

When I get caught in a negative belief, I take a deep breath and focus on something positive or something I'm proud of.

This habit, along with meditation every morning, has helped me profoundly.

A wise mentor once told me that negative thoughts are like speeding cars on a freeway. Observe them, watch them, and let them pass.

The alternative is to get caught up in them, allow them to create stress in your life, and create a chain reaction of negativity.

How To Make Your Brain Happy

IF YOU'RE LIKE me, you're interested in being happier, more focused, and more successful.

And if your brain is like mine, it is constantly dwelling on negative thoughts.

These negative thoughts quite literally shrink your brain and can breed a host of physical and mental problems.

It's this understanding that literally forced me into the habit of meditation, and the results have been nothing short of amazing. My sense of connectedness and clarity of mind has been life changing to say the least.

The brain controls how we feel, the decisions we make, and how others feel about us. And today, I'm going to show you the #1 thing you can do to completely change your brain – physiologically and psychologically — for the better.

So, let's dive right into the "life changing secret" of mindfulness and meditation.

Mindfulness is a non-judgmental awareness of your moment-to -moment experience.

There is no *good* or *bad*, there just is, and it's all part of your awareness.

Mindfulness prevents you from living deep in your negative thoughts and puts you out on this wonderful miracle of life.

It teaches you to accept and adapt to anything and everything life throws at you.

This is important because your thoughts are your energy – they control your "vibes" – and your energy is important for business, dating, quality of life, and everything in-between.

When you become more mindful, not only are you "in the moment," you're happier and more focused.

So, how do we achieve this amazing state of mindfulness?

It's quite simple.

Meditation.

Meditation is the practice that forces your brain to become more mindful, shifts negative thinking, and helps overcome stress and depression.

Many people put meditation in the "woooo-saaah" hippie stuff category, but it's far from it. Just like lifting weights at the gym makes your muscles stronger, meditation makes your brain stronger (it literally changes the physiology of your brain).

It's almost a must to living a superior quality of life.

And the best part is you can build a successful meditation habit in just ten minutes a day.

How?

Download the HeadSpace app to your iPhone (it's free). They offer an introduction to meditation course – ten days, for ten minutes a day. Andy, the charming British founder of the company, will walk you through meditation, step by step.

Ten days was all it took for me to see the crazy benefits and adopt this life-changing habit.

Ten minutes is all you need.

I recommend doing it first thing in the morning, before your mind gets polluted and you *"don't have the time."*

This is truly the most low investment thing you can do that will yield the biggest benefits.

I don't even notice the benefits of meditation anymore.

BUT, when I skip my daily meditation?

I sure as hell feel the chaotic, negative and anxiety-ridden nature of my brain. And it makes me wonder how I could ever live without meditation and a calm mind.

If you want to feel instantly, become happier, more focused, and "present," do yourself a favor and download the HeadSpace app.

I can't recommend this practice enough.

"Meditate for an hour every day unless you are too busy. In that case meditate for two hours."
Zen Proverb

How To Sleep Like A Boss

A GOOD NIGHT of sleep isn't only good for the purpose of waking up early and getting more done.

It's absolutely necessary for your health and the improvement of your daily life.

Your body (and brain, of course) literally recharge themselves when you sleep.

For example, your body produces most of your Growth Hormone (or GH for short) during sleep. GH controls how much fat you burn, how much muscle you build, your sex drive and motivation, and it keeps your immune system and mental faculties running smoothly.

Lack of quality sleep will not only slow the production of GH, it will increase the production of Cortisol. This is a stress hormone that promotes fat storage, kills your muscles, hurts your immune system, and the worst part — it puts you in a stressed-out-and can't-handle-your-life kind of mood.

Basically, lack of quality sleep means...

...your body will store more fat...

...your muscles will shrink...

...your sex drive will decrease...

...you'll be in a terrible mood.

So, now that we've gotten the importance of a quality sleep out of the way, let's talk about making an effort to get to bed earlier and get a solid 6 to 9 hours of sleep so we can wake up feeling amazing.

The first thing you'll want to do is avoid any caffeine or stimulants 6 to 8 hours before your target bedtime.

You'll also want to avoid blue light, using a program like flux for your computer or getting a blue-light blocking screen protector for your phone.

Next, you'll want to set aside some "thinking" time to plan out what you want to accomplish the next day. Make sure to write down everything that's on your mind. This will also act as a sort of "brain dump" so you won't be thinking about all that needs to be done while you're unplugging from the world and getting ready to doze off. Make sure to end your writing session with a positive message for yourself.

From there, you'll want to pour up a cup of some calming chamomile tea. Or if you really have trouble falling asleep, supplement with 3mg of Melatonin.

Now, you'll want to dim the lights and darken the house, giving your brain the signal that it's time to sleep

I'm not a fan of having any bulky technology—computer, television, etc—in the same room where I sleep.

If you can, lower the room temperature a little bit, I like to sleep at 69 Fahrenheit. During a deep sleep, your body temperature drops, so sleeping a cooler room is definitely helpful.

Now that everything is in place, take a few deep breaths, wind down, and let your mind wander with some light fiction until you doze off.

This nightly routine will help you get a deeper sleep, wake up earlier, and have more energy throughout the day — which will only be conducive to your success in life.

It's 6:42 a.m right now as I write this lesson.

I've found that I'm much more effective going to bed before 11 p.m. It allows me to wake up early and get most of my work done before most of my friends are even awake.

The Morning Holy Hour

IF YOU'RE LIKE most people, getting out of bed in the morning isn't exactly the most awesome thing ever.

And I get it. Trust me.

But what if I told you that for some, the morning is the most important part of the day?

A time for inner peace, uninterrupted productivity, and self-reflection.

Winners know that getting a head start in the calmest hours of the day provides a momentum that carries on throughout the entire day.

And it's not just about being more productive and getting more done. Studies show that morning people are happier and more proactive (on the contrary – night owls are classified as more intelligent and productive).

See, while most people are hitting the snooze button in bed, or fumbling to put their pants on and rush out the door, you have an opportunity to set the stage for an amazing day by exploiting the morning holy hour.

The morning holy hour is 60 minutes to stimulate the mind, nourish the body, and develop your character.

It involves getting up early to do some internal work and letting all of that carry on with you through your day.

This holy hour actually starts the night before, though.

If you haven't already read the previous lesson, *How To Sleep Like A Boss*, you'll want to read that before continuing.

All caught up? Alright, this is how you create a morning holy hour:

Avoid Anything That Disconnects You From Yourself

Don't wake up and:

1. Check your phone

2. Check your email

3. Interact in any way with social media

4. Turn on the TV or watch YouTube

5. Do anything that will either numb you, or produce anxiety.

Work Your Body

Just 10-15 minutes of focused exercise in the morning is all you need to reap the positive benefits. Do you know how good it feels to be done with your exercise before people even wake up?

The cascade of endorphins and blood flow from your workout translates into positive thoughts that last throughout the day, not to mention the energy boost and mental edge to swiftly deal with anything that comes your way.

There's no better way to start the day.

Work Your Mind

As little as ten minutes of meditation will provide an amazing calm and clarity that will last throughout the day.

Learn Something

Read anything that inspires you, stimulates you, or gives you an edge in your industry. Reading in the morning (ideally with your coffee) puts new thoughts and ideas into your head. Read about something or somebody you're interested in. All it takes is one idea in one book to completely change your life. And at the very least, you'll have something interesting to talk about with strangers.

Write Something

Write about anything you want – the day ahead, your goals, lessons learned, anything.

The point is to articulate your thoughts and hone your writing skills, which is a pretty damn valuable skill, if I do say so myself.

I use this cool service called MailDiary.net that emails me every morning and asks me to write about the day. The e-mail includes a random entry from the past. It shows me progress not only in my writing, but in my personal development.

I've seen many goals manifested into reality through my journal. It's a pretty sweet way to keep records and track your life progress, as well as notice patterns in your life and learn from your mistakes.

Plus, it's kinda fun and therapeutic talking to yourself.

Nourish Your Body

Instead of spending time cooking, or slowing yourself down by eating a big meal, prepare a super-food shake or drink a green juice to fuel your body and mind.

Make sure you drink a lot of water too. Our brains are 85 percent water, so this is crucial. Studies show that water makes you smarter and your moods more stable.

If you can start your morning with good habits, healthy clarity, and self-care, these qualities will follow you around through the day.

You'll be charged in your body, mind, and spirit, and ready to do much more at a higher functioning level in less time.

THE POWER OF GRATITUDE

THE BENEFITS OF expressing gratitude are nearly endless.

In fact, many people say gratitude the key to happiness.

Consciously expressing gratitude puts you in the space to appreciate all that is good in life.

The alternative is to use your mental energy to think about all the things you wish you had, etc.

Here's some perspective.

If you woke up breathing, you're incredibly blessed.

Sometimes it takes a tragedy to remind you of what's really important in life.

For me, gratitude reminds me every day of what's really important. It shows me what makes me happy, and gets my brain focused on all the goodness in life.

I was reading a book called *Thanks! How The New Science Of Gratitude Can Make You Happier*. The author, a UC Davis Psychologist, shows studies of people who keep gratitude journals. He goes on to show that these people experience more positive emotions, feel more alive, sleep better, express more compassion and kindness, and even have stronger immune systems.

The conclusion? Regularly writing brief reflections on the things you're thankful for can significantly increase your quality of life.

I do this along with a daily journal — a self assessment of sorts — where I can write down what went well for the day and what I can do to make it even better next time.

This forces me to be aware about how I'm spending my time and energy, and it also keeps me on track towards my goals.

The thing is, though , writing in the gratitude journal can become repetitive. I mean, how many times can I write that I'm grateful for my morning coffee and the sun shining on my skin (spoiler: a lot of times)?

This book helped teach me a few tricks to maintain my gratitude practice over the long haul.

1. Switch Things Up

The key to reaping the benefits of gratitude is to constantly notice new things you're thankful for every day.

Today, I'm grateful that I'm getting paid to research gratitude and then share that knowledge with everyone here.

You must keep your brain alert to recognizing opportunities for gratitude by writing about specific daily things you're thankful for.

2. Don't Force It

Don't write in your gratitude journal because you "have to do it." Make time for it when it best fits your schedule.

For me, that's mornings when my brain is fresh, uninterrupted, and fired up off coffee.

The key here is to integrate this into your life smoothly and painlessly — not stress out and add another thing to your to-do list.

3. Be Social

Our relationships are often the greatest factor affecting our happiness.

The author of the book I mentioned above suggests that

you should express gratitude for people, rather than circumstances or material items. He goes as far as recommending you include others in your expression of gratitude.

If you're feeling grateful for someone, let that person know.

Here's an exercise you can do right now:

Send a text to someone you haven't spoken to in a long time and let them know that you're thinking about them, and are grateful for the memories you share with that person. Bonus points if you can be specific about a moment you shared with that person.

4. Don't Complicate It

Express gratitude however you prefer.

For me, I write in a paper journal each day. I just list things I'm grateful for after my morning writing prompt. It gives me a nice boost for the rest of the day.

I'll never forget this lesson a mentor drilled into my head:

Get yourself in a great mood before you start working and dealing with people.

WHAT IS IT WITH THIS FITNESS THING?

WHY DO SOME people live in fear of it, while others can't seem to live without it?

And why is it that the happiest and most successful people in the world love fitness, and can't function without it?

In this lesson, I set out to figure out these questions.

As a society, we tend to judge the overweight.

They're lazy.

They lack self-control.

They have no self-respect.

They eat too much fucking ice cream.

And most of the time, our assumptions are right. Everyone is capable of taking action and creating a better life for themselves. Playing the victim to your circumstances usually indicates a lack of internal motivation for a better life, and a fear of change.

Usually a bit of both.

Oh well, they say. I'll start tomorrow, they say.

I'll just have one spoonful of ice cream this time. Two bites. Three bites. The whole tub?

It's a vicious cycle of bad habits and poor self-care, and sadly, too many people accept this lower standard of living as their mere existence.

So, to understand, let's define the word fitness:

The ability to carry out daily tasks (work and play) with vigor and alertness, without undue fatigue and with ample energy to enjoy leisure-time pursuits and to meet unforeseen emergencies (Clarke 1976).

Sounds like it makes us more awesome, right?

Now, let's break down about 50% of this fitness thing, and define the world exercise:

Exercise: Activity requiring physical effort.

You should make it a priority to do some kind of activity for at least 20 minutes a day. I like to work out in the morning as it gets my juices flowing, but it's completely subjective.

Now that we have that out of the way, let's get right into the three reasons you should exercise right now.

Reason #1 Exercise Makes You Happy

Have you every heard of somebody that regretted a workout? There's no doubt about the relationship between exercising and being awesome.

Countless studies show that exercise is known to improve moods, lower depression, boost self-esteem, reduce stress/anxiety, improve your sleep quality and your sex life.

One study even suggested that high intensity exercise stimulates the brain the same way cocaine does – without the nasty side effects.

When you put your body though intense exercise, your brain produces natural feel good chemicals called endorphins. They're often described as euphoric and are also released during sex and laughter.

You'll almost always walk out of the gym in a better mood than you walked in.

Reason #2 Exercise Makes You Smart

Not exercising means less brain activity, and less ability for you to achieve and succeed in anything.

A study done on over 6,000 people showed that those with more fat experienced 22% more cognitive decline than those who were at a normal weight.

That means being out of shape not only slows your body down, it slows down your brain as well.

There's no shortage of research that shows a positive connection between exercise and the brain.

Exercise accelerates our Brain-Derived Neurotropic Factor. BDNF is an important hormone that controls how we learn things and how much activity we have going on in our brains. It's often referred to as "Miracle-Gro for the brain" by Professors of Psychiatry at Harvard.

It's no wonder why a billionaire entrepreneur like Richard Branson claims his number one 'secret' to productivity is exercise. He runs over 400 companies and exercises daily.

He's also 66 old. What was your excuse again?

Reason #3 Exercise Makes You Sexy

Of course, looking great naked is a huge benefit and a perfectly fine reason to exercise.

But exercise makes us sexy in so many other ways.

It teaches us the process of achieving anything worthwhile in life:

Goal Setting -> Planning -> Deadline -> Commitment -> Discipline -> Accomplishment -> Satisfaction -> Bigger Goal -> Repeat

By achieving our fitness goals, we reinforce the idea that if we set a goal and work toward it, the outcome will be positive.

And just like that we've increased our self worth and built the rock solid confidence that's needed to take on anything in our way and create the best life possible for ourselves.

Fitness is not just about burning calories or looking better naked (although those are important).

It's about a million perks that make your life better. It's about loving yourself (but not in a narcissistic douche-bag kind of way).

Fitness is a celebration of a healthy body and mind, and you should be celebrating everyday.

Are You Burnt Out?

I'VE BEEN EXPERIENCING burnout lately.

I've overextended myself and am juggling multiple writing and consulting gigs, while trying to finally publish this book.

Burnout is different from stress.

It lingers.

And sneaks up on you out of nowhere.

Burnout has been hurting my relationships --- romantic ones, personal ones, and professional ones.

It's hard to love others when you don't love yourself, and burnout definitely affects your self worth and how you feel about yourself.

Today's lesson is about identifying the symptoms of burnout so you can prevent it from sneaking up on you.

While researching for this lesson, I came across something called the Maslach Burnout Inventory, which is the scientific framework for identifying burnout.

The MBI defines burnout as *"a psychological syndrome of emotional exhaustion, depersonalization, and reduced personal accomplishment that can occur among individuals who work with other people in some capacity."*

Everyone is susceptible to burnout, and here are the three biggest symptoms:

Emotional Exhaustion

This is the feeling of being emotionally overextended, drained, and overwhelmed by your work.

The MBI defines emotional exhaustion as *no longer being able to give yourself to work or others at a psychological level.*

Depersonalization

This is the development of negative and cynical attitudes towards your colleagues and clients.

The MBI shows that this is caused by emotional exhaustion.

Reduced Personal Accomplishment

This is when you start to develop negative feelings towards yourself.

This shows up as poor self-esteem, low self-efficacy, and overall downplaying your abilities. In spite of all of your accomplishments, you're still upset about your skills, and where you are in your career.

Usually, just one of these symptoms triggers a negative cascade of the others. It's an ugly cycle, and it only accelerates itself.

According to the MBI, there are six risk factors that lead to burnout:

1. **Workload:** Having too much work, with too little resources (including time).
2. **Control:** Being micromanaged or not having enough influence or meaning in your work.
3. **Reward:** Working for not enough pay, not receiving enough acknowledgement, or feeling little satisfaction towards your work.
4. **Community:** Working in isolation and experiencing conflict or disrespect with those around you.
5. **Fairness:** Being discriminated against or falling on the short end of the stick in regards to favoritism.
6. **Values:** Having ethical conflicts with the work or completing meaningless tasks

It's worth noting that you don't have to have all of those risk factors to experience burnout. I'd only experienced two (community and reward), and still started to feel burnout creeping up on me.

Burnout is different from "stress," because burnout is a chronic condition, which means it is constant and ongoing.

But the good news is that burnout is preventable. You can...

...take a [long] break from work... ...talk to people and seek help (coaching, mastermind groups, anything)...

...have that uncomfortable conversation with your boss...

...or, if you're brave, leave your job.

If that scares you, you should start working on your side hustle first while planning your exit strategy from your job – more on that later in this book.

Burnout isn't just uncomfortable, it's the enemy of happiness.

When you first notice the symptoms, it's time to unplug and take a deep look at your current situation. There is a serious power in unplugging.

What helps me the most with combating the symptoms of burnout is:

1. Working on my meaningful side hustle and personal writing projects.
2. Unplugging from technology and work and getting lost in nature.
3. Hitting the gym and playing basketball (aggressively).
4. Meditating and journaling

Sometimes all you need to do is honor "you time" after one great night of sleep.

THE NOT TO DO LIST

THIS LESSON IS about self-improvement through simplification.

It's about removing distractions, identifying time killers, and spending your time with the most essential things in your life.

What are your essentials?

For me, it's my friends and family, my work, and self mastery.

Self mastery, for me, is reading, writing, meditating, journaling, eating healthy, creating art, and working out.

I've identified those as the things that make my quality of life better, and I make sure to give them time every single day.

When you spend most of your time on your essentials, you'll get much more out of your life. You'll see your moods become increasingly positive, your relationships will be more enjoyable, and you'll begin excelling at whatever it is you're focused on.

Now, I've told you my essentials. It's time for you to discover your own.

Give yourself 10 minutes and list 4-5 activities that make you feel great.

Now that you have those, you need to identify your time killers.

Time killers are the things that take away time from your essentials.

For me, time killers include mindlessly surfing the internet or indulging in distracting entertainment – like funny videos on Instagram.

I like to monitor how I spend my time every night when I recap my day in my journal. This makes me aware of my bad habits and time-killers.

I want you to give yourself another 10 minutes, and really list all the things you spend your time with each day. Compare that list with your 4-5 essentials list you made earlier.

What could you change in order to have more time for your

essentials?

This is about ruthless elimination of the non-essentials and protection of your most valuable asset – your time.

That's how you move forward with what's important to you.

TAKE TIME TO THINK

WHEN YOU WORK smart, you work on the things that matter.

You work on the things that move you toward your goals.

And you can't work smart without dedicating time to think.

Warren Buffett is the CEO of the fourth largest company in the United States, and has arguably one of the world's most successful business records. By his own estimate, he has spent over 80% of his career reading, and thinking.

Warren Buffett keeps his schedule wide open.

This is absolutely counter-intuitive to what we think a successful CEO does, and especially with all the "rah rah" work harder and hustle gospel being spread around today.

Naturally, we are going to assume that Warren Buffet is an anomaly, and we'd be absolutely correct to think that. But in the past few years, this approach to strategy and uninterrupted thinking has gained popularity.

For example, Tim Armstrong, the CEO of AOL, makes his executives spend four hours per week just thinking.

Jeff Weiner, CEO of LinkedIn, schedules two hours of uninterrupted thinking time each day.

And even Bill Gates is known to take a week off twice a year just to reflect deeply without interruption.

And I do the same – every morning, before I turn on my phone or computer, I spend 30 uninterrupted minutes just drinking my cup of coffee and thinking. From there, I meditate for ten minutes and then journal my thoughts.

It's a great way to get clarity in your life. For me, it serves as a sort of 'inventory check' of where I'm at now and where I'm going.

Now, aside from carving out some time to think, you should have some intentions going into this time.

Here are a few powerful questions to ask yourself:

1. Am I doing the right things with the right people?
2. What's most important to me?
3. What am I good at?
4. What am I bad at?
5. How can I spend more time doing what I'm good at?

6. How can I spend less time doing what I'm bad at?

Alternately, you can write down a goal and think about how you will strategically move toward it.

And use your constant thinking time to monitor yourself and adjust your strategy as you move forward.

Daily uninterrupted thinking serves as a sort of accountability check' and reminder — are you moving toward what's important to you?

PATIENCE IS A VIRTUE

YOU DON'T NEED to have your life figured out just yet.

We all spend way too much time worrying about the future and what we are supposed to be doing.

This takes us away from the only thing we actually have control over — the present.

We are stuck in a trap that lets us believe we should be exactly where we think we should be.

Where we have everything figured out, and we're on the top of the mountain, basking in all the glory of life and our success.

What we forget is: we are exactly where we need to be in life.

If something hasn't happened for you, it just means you're not ready.

It means you're getting the experience you need so you can kill it when you are ready.

That is, if you ever are ready.

And you will be ready IF you do this one thing:

Make a commitment to lifelong learning and growing.

It's a matter of constantly learning what part of you is missing that will allow you to achieve everything you want in life.

The major lesson is to be patient.

You have your whole life to become and create as long as you're aware, moving forward, and learning.

You're on exactly the right path.

It's absolutely okay to not have life figured out.

There is a major difference between laziness and procrastination, with the majority of procrastination being caused by a fear of failure.

It's easy to see others' success, compare yourself, and feel bad.

But instead, you should realize that as long as you're taking action, learning, and moving forward, you're exactly where you need to be in life.

Here's a list of patient people at the top of their game:

At age 23, Oprah was fired from her first reporting job.

At age 24, Stephen King was working as a janitor and living in a trailer.

At age 27, Vincent Van Gogh failed as a missionary and decided to go to art school.

At age 28, J.K. Rowling was a suicidal single parent living on welfare.

At age 30, Harrison Ford was a carpenter.

At age 30, Martha Stewart was a stockbroker.

Christian Dior founded Dior at the age of 41.

Jerry Baldwin founded Starbucks at 42.

Alan Rickman gave up his graphic design career and landed his first movie role at age 42.

Steve Carrel got his big break at age 43.

Stan Lee didn't release his first big comic book until he was

43.

Samuel L. Jackson didn't get his first major movie role until he was 46.

Charles Darwin published *The Origin Of Species* at age 50.

Morgan Freeman landed his first major movie role at age 52.

Kathryn Bigelow won the Academy Award for Best Director when she made The Hurt Locker at age 57.

Winston Churchill struggled in politics and was defeated in every election until the age of 62 when he became Prime Minister of the UK.

Colonel Sanders founded KFC at age 65.

This game of life is a marathon, not a sprint.

SECTION II: CONFIDENCE

CAN MONEY BUY HAPPINESS?

YOU ALL KNOW the cliché "money can't buy happiness."

But is it true? Or it something touted by broke people?

Personally, I think it's misguided.

For example --- being materialistic and buying more things doesn't make me happy.

Sure, acquiring new things comes with a sugar high, and some status signaling benefits (which can help you land new business or a hot date).

But it's a temporary sugar high that fades away – if you're looking to materials for happiness.

There are many different [weak] studies about money that hold two sides to the argument. But the baseline is this: After your necessities are covered (average is around $40k/ year) more money barely makes you happier.

65

When you have the basics covered, things like health, relationships, and a sense of purpose matter far more than money.

Again, these studies are all weak, and I'd be more interested in hearing directly from you.

Does having more money make you happier? How much?

For me, being rich means freedom (and more money means more freedom). More money means I have more time to enjoy my lifestyle, work on what matters to me, and have the resources to go on adventures around the world and learn new things.

One study I read while researching for this lesson said that while money doesn't buy happiness, money buys experiences. And experiences bring happiness.

And I couldn't agree more.

Time: Your Most Valuable Asset

THERE'S A MYTH that time is money.

But in fact, time is even more precious than money.

It's a nonrenewable resource. Once you've spent it, and if you've spent it badly, it's gone forever.

The above is a quote from Dr. Neil Fiore.

Your biggest asset is your time because you can never get it back.

And the biggest time waster today is...

Social Media.

It's a blessing and a curse. While allowing us to stay connected to those we care about, it has also created a massive attention and perception problem.

Social media is designed to be addictive, and it stimulates

the same part of your brain as cocaine – your dopamine receptors.

The result is a society of drones that have left the real world behind in an attempt to embrace the false perception of a virtual world.

Just go outside on a beautiful day and watch these zombies locked into their phones – oblivious to the beauty around them.

These people are not present; they are not living in the moment.

The worst part of this, though, is not only the false perception of the world around us, but the amount of time we waste here.

It's become the norm to spend hours checking all of your social media. And this is often taking us away from becoming our best selves and performing at our highest capacity.

You need to understand that social media is not a necessity in your life, but only a small supplement to it.

Here are a few ways to take your time back without being that weird guy without a Facebook:

Delete The FaceBook App From Your Phone

Or at the very least disable the push notifications.

These apps are designed to be addictive and stimulate your dopamine receptors, and each notification is like an invitation back to the time-wasting party.

Get Rid Of Your Newsfeed

If you're like me and randomly log onto Facebook every few minutes to see what's on the feed, you need this app.

Download Newsfeed Eradicator – It replaces your newsfeed with a motivational quote.

Use Self Control

For your most important tasks, download this app. It completely blocks out sites of your choosing for a set amount of time (and there's no way to reverse it).

I use it when writing.

Track Your Time

What gets measured gets managed.

Download an app called "RescueTime" onto your computer.

See where you spend most of your time online.

This app showed me that I was wasting around 2 hours per day on Facebook, which shocked me and inspired this lesson.

Batch Your Social Media

Dedicate a set hour to check all of your social media once per day.

This requires a bit of discipline but is the most valuable tip of them all.

I highly recommend taking this lesson seriously – especially if you're like me and at the end of some "productive" days, you wonder to yourself:

What the fuck did I accomplish today, really?

Try this for one month and see how much more productive you are.

Screw Your To Do List

LET'S BE REAL for a second.

You have a to-do list.

And it's always left undone.

Now, you feel overwhelmed, busy, unproductive, and even depressed.

Well that's all about to change.

This lesson is a big SCREW YOU to your to do list.

Last week, I was reading a book called *Willpower: Rediscovering The Greatest Human Strength*.

A study in the book showed that a person has at least 150 different tasks at a time, and sometimes a to-do list for a single Monday could take more than a week to finish.

Sounds like a recipe for failure.

Filling up our to-do lists creates a constant turmoil in our heads and has a negative effect on actually getting those tasks done.

In *Willpower*, the authors discovered that "worry" comes from having too many conflicting goals.

This causes our productivity as well as our physical and mental health to suffer.

Can you relate? I definitely can.

Here are a few more reasons why it's time to ditch the to-do list:

#1 They don't account for how long something will take.

Let's be real. We're really bad at gauging the time required to complete the task. As a result, we all put more things on our list than we are capable of doing.

#2 They Lack Clarity

There is no difference between urgent and important. There are no time boundaries. And we tend to "do" the urgent tasks and put off the most important ones.

#3 They Lack Schedule

Unless you're a badass, your to-do list is probably just a set of randomly gathered tasks in no particular order.

When you start your workday, you usually pick the ones based on your current mood.

And when there is no schedule, you're more than likely to start switching between a few.

This also leads to procrastination.

Overall, the to-do List gives you the illusion of progress and accomplishment.

But I believe that to-do lists make you prioritize the wrong stuff and make you less organized in the long run.

But planning and productivity are such an important ingredient in success.

So what to do?

Schedule Everything Rigorously

Be a professional. Write down your tasks, and dedicate time to them.

And stick to that schedule.

Give Yourself Tight Deadlines

The longer your deadline, the more likely you are to waste time and procrastinate.

Prioritize

Schedule your most important tasks in the morning.

Start your day by doing your most important thing, and use that momentum to carry you through the rest of your day.

Be Real With Yourself

Don't overwork yourself. Don't schedule more tasks than you can handle.

Hard work has nothing to do with productivity.

Your journey to success begins with you prioritizing, and executing what's important for you.

The worst thing you can do is burn yourself out.

Your health and energy will take you everywhere you want to go.

Mental Toughness

WHAT MAKES A bigger impact than talent or intelligence?

Mental toughness.

Research is starting to reveal that mental toughness is the most important factor for achieving your goals in health, in business, and in life.

That's great news because you can't do much about the genes you're born with, but you can do a lot to develop mental toughness.

Mental toughness is defined as your perseverance to achieve long-term goals.

This is all about your perspective.

Can you keep your life together after the woman you thought was the love of your life leaves you for another man?

Will you bounce back after your business goes bankrupt?

If you got fired today, would you be able to find a better job a.s.a.p.?

Mental toughness is about how we respond to extreme situations Mental toughness is a muscle, that should be worked often, to grow and develop.

It's strengthened through MOTION.

Not meditation.

You can read hundreds of books on your Kindle, but the only way to develop mental toughness is by TAKING ACTION.

Mental toughness isn't about motivation or inspiration – that stuff is fickle, and they come and go.

Mental toughness is about habits – the ones necessary for you to achieve your goals. And it's about keeping those habits consistent. Even when you don't feel like it.

Usually, when things get tough, people simply find something easier to work on.

Mental toughness is about your dedication to a goal and your ability to stick to a consistent schedule.

No matter what life throws your way.

How To Develop Mental Toughness

WE ALL HAVE this mental toughness deep inside of us. The problem is that we have become disconnected from this inner power because of social conditioning, and a host of other environmental factors.

So here are a few reminders and guidelines for owning your inner power today:

#1 Stop Proving

You have nothing to prove.

No need to please, pretend, or protect in order to justify yourself.

You are you. Own it.

Everyone respects the person who is proud of his beliefs, no matter how weird or different those beliefs may be.

#2 Be More Curious

Listen intently to someone when they speak to you.

Look at the world with the eyes of a child.

Ask more questions and engage in dialogue.

Beautiful opportunities will open up for you if you are curious about all that is around you.

#3 Look To The Company You Keep

You are the average of the five people you spend the most time with.

Yes, you've heard this a million times, and it's true.

We tend to absorb and reflect the attitudes of the people around us – it's our human nature.

Who you spend time with has a huge impact on how you see yourself and how you feel about yourself.

Are the people you're with building you up, or bringing you down?

#4 Stop Wishing

Just fucking take action and work toward what you want.

Mindset is everything.

#5 Play To Your Strengths

Whatever you're good at, do more of it.

If you're not sure, then get curious — deeply curious — about yourself.

Pay attention until you start noticing.

Think about how you would spend your day if you could do anything you wanted.

Now, make the time for yourself, and go do some of those things.

#6 Avoid The Comfort Zone

This is the danger zone.

You go into it and immediately go blind to what's really happening.

Magic doesn't happen in the comfort zone. It happens in the places that force growth – the risky, uncomfortable places.

When we stop growing, we shrink and get left behind.

Confidence comes from stepping out of the comfort zone.

#7 Trust Your Full Intelligence

Intelligence is not just about your brain. Your intuition and your emotions, even your gut – are all forms of intelligence.

We may not be able to logically understand something or prove it with facts, but that doesn't mean it's not real.

Pay attention to hunches or gut instincts.

Deepen your connection to your intuition and that inner whisper that tells you what's right and what's not.

That inner voice is a superpower.

Harness it.

#8 Know You Are Ready

So many people are always waiting, waiting, first this, then that...

The truth is you're 100% ready right now.

The time will never be perfect and the only way is to get started.

Right now.

If You're The Smartest Person In The Room...

IF SO, YOU'RE in the wrong room.

You already know the maxim "you are the average of the 5 people you spend your time with."

And that statement couldn't be truer.

Not only does your immediate network affect your energy and mindset, it also controls your perceptions and standards for what is possible in life.

Surrounding yourself with people smarter and more successful than you is one of the most powerful ways to absorb some of their expertise and help you get where you're trying to go.

Mastermind groups have successfully been able to kick my ass into gear, help me change my mindset and perspective on challenges in my life, as well as network and learn from entrepreneurs I respect.

Whether it's a paid mastermind, conference, or group of smart friends you can have powerful conversations with, creating an environment where you're not the smartest person in the room will have a massive impact on your life.

I make it a priority to attend at least one conference every 3 months. That's non-negotiable for me.

It helps with my personal and professional development, my commitment to my craft, and also, it helps me grow my network and meet very smart, wealthy, and influential individuals.

I've been blessed with the opportunity to have some powerful mentors, and I know that's not available to everyone. However, if you're looking to find a mentor, here are a few tips one of my mentors wanted me to share with you:

1. Be capable of taking advice and learning. Don't defend wrong behaviors or try to prove yourself. Just be a great student.

2. Be non-judgmental and non-threatening.

3. Be willing to add value and expect nothing in return. Be of service, and success will find you.

5. Be around people more successful than yourself.

If you're the smartest person in the room, you're in the wrong room.

Do whatever it takes to get in rooms with people more skilled or smarter than yourself, and soak it all in.

How To Make People Like You

"CHARISMA GETS PEOPLE to like you, trust you, and want to be led by you. It can determine whether you're seen as a follower or a leader, whether your ideas get adopted, and how effectively your projects are implemented" - Olivia Fox Cabane, *The Charisma Myth*

Charisma can be broken down into these three components:

The Way You Act

You want to communicate your value to the world through your actions.

Confident, strong, calm, and intelligent.

You have the courage to stand up for yourself and your values.

You're not afraid to tell things the way they really are, with a level of sensitivity.

You're an optimist with a brutal realism, and maintaining a solid reputation is important to you.

You have high standards for your life, but you display them humbly.

The Way You Look

This is the easiest and most important part.

You should look clear and polished – haircut, facial hair, nail, teeth, and yes, body odor, should be at their best at all times.

No need to be a gym freak, but you should at least appear "fit" and "healthy."

You could be the best-looking guy in the room, but if you're wearing a dirty, over-sized, yellowing t-shirt and shorts that hang like bells around your thighs, that won't matter much.

Similarly, you could be the worst-looking guy in the room, but if you are looking sharp and polished, with a well thought out outfit that suits you perfectly, people are going to want to align with you.

The great news is that this is all something that is in your control. Anyone reading this can put in the effort to look amazing.

The Way You Communicate

You should speak slowly and confidently.

When you talk to new people, you can focus on first establishing your value and an emotional connection through talking about something personal, a shared experience, or using positive humor. This will make you instantly more likable.

Use your emotional intelligence to blend in by mirroring your speech, energy, and communication modalities to whomever you are communicating with.

And keep your body language relaxed but powerful at all times.

Your posture not only signals to the world your level of confidence, but it actually has psychological effects that influence how you feel about yourself.

How To Tell A Good Story

TODAY'S LESSON IS about the act of storytelling – to impress and attract partners, customers, or even your boss.

Humans are wired to respond to stories; it's in our nature.

Advertisers understand this and use stories to sell you things.

Simply put: if you can tell a good story, the kind that has people hanging onto your every word, and anticipating the next, you have a superpower in your hands.

A recent study published in the scientific journal, *Personal Relationships*, suggests that people portrayed as stronger storytellers are considered higher status than those that aren't — and this status will make you appear more romantically attractive (amongst other benefits that come with having 'high status'). The men who were better storytellers were voted as attractive and seen as better quality for becoming a romantic partner.

Pretty interesting stuff coming out of the world of evolutionary psychology...

But story telling isn't only about seducing a partner. Telling good stories gives you power.

If you can command attention, you have power – whether that is social power at a cocktail party, or influential power at a business meeting.

In today's hyper-connected world, where everyone is competing for attention 24/7, the ability to tell a good story (the kind that commands attention) separates you.

It gives you command over others.

If you can get people to give you their undivided time, energy, and attention … well, you can get them to do almost anything.

Whether you're at the bar or club, on a date, or at a professional networking event, telling stories allows you to capture attention and get your point across in a way that will be remembered.

So, here are the four steps to successful story-telling:

1. Inject Emotion

The whole point of telling a story is to create an emotional connection between you and the listener (or reader).

Every story has an emotional core, and that core comes down to how you feel about the events you are describing.

You need emotion to make your story compelling, and to get people hooked.

When thinking of the story you want to tell, think back to how you felt.

What was motivating you? What troubled you? How did you feel about it all?

The more emotion you inject, the better.

But your story doesn't have to be a dramatic soap opera. Simply saying something like "I couldn't believe it" or "at this point, I was absolutely terrified" is enough to inject emotion and get people hooked into your story.

Remember, you have to be interested to be interesting.

2. Know The Narrative

Every story is simply a series of events that need to be described in the right order.

Extra information will just slow people down, take them out of the flow of your story, and have them wondering what the point is.

You must carve out the essentials to your story and stick to them.

While every story is different, most follow a general pattern.

Most stories start with a quick background to get the listener ready.

From there you dive into the story, usually with a hook, something that commands attention from the opening.

Then you tell the events of your story, building up tension until the dramatic peak, the point of no return – also known as the climax.

You then go into the final events of the story, and the lessons learned and consequences of the story. This is called the denouement, and is the end of your story.

Following this general pattern is crucial to being a good storyteller.

3. Practice The Craft

You ever hear a great story from someone?

It draws you in. It builds tension. And the storyteller is

delivering every single thing right on cue.

This storyteller probably has the pauses just right.

It's not by chance.

Good storytellers practice their craft, and often.

Whether it's at Toastmasters, or practicing with friends or strangers – the more you tell, the better you will get.

The rewards of being a good storyteller will provide you with one of the most powerful skills in life – the ability to make emotional connections with others.

Get started by practicing with me right now.

Email me at slando@gmail.com and tell me your best personal story.

Remember to keep out the extra information, stick to the general narrative pattern, and inject lots of emotion.

How To Make People Support And Share Your Ideas

WHETHER YOU'RE A businessman, politician, musician, or artist – your success depends on your ability to get your ideas to spread to large amounts of people.

But how do you get them to pay attention to your ideas?

And how do you get people to share your message and actually care about it?

Jonah Berger, marketing professor and author of *Contagious*, does a great job at this.

He studies word of mouth, social influence, and viral marketing.

His book reveals the common recipes behind good ideas and is based on the latest research in psychology, and is backed up by insightful case studies.

Here are the 6 biggest takeaways I got from the book. The more your idea fits this recipe, the more likely it is to be successful.

Takeaway #1

Social Currency

We share things to look good.

We often share information because it shows we are "in the know."

When your idea is backed by social currency, it means there is value to sharing it with others.

It signals that we are knowledgeable, sexy, funny, or "cool."

The idea is quite simple: if sharing your idea or product makes people feel better about themselves (if it adds a social benefit), people are gong to be more likely to share it.

Not because they love you, but because they love themselves.

Takeaway #2

Triggers

We share things when we are triggered to do so by

something in the environment.

The more we are reminded of something, the more likely we are to share it.

This is why marketers know that it usually takes at least 7 communications to get someone to buy your stuff.

And here are some crazy examples of how triggers work:

In 1997, the candy company Mars experienced a spike in sales, even though they hadn't changed anything about their marketing.

The reason? NASA had just started a mission to Mars, and it was being reported all over the news. The simple triggers of "Mars" influenced more people to buy the candy bar.

Another example is The Kit Kat Bar.

In 2007 they launched a marketing campaign to link Kit Kats and coffee, describing the pair as "a break's best friend."

The campaign was very successful – sales increased and the $300 million dollar brand grew into a $500 million brand.

This was another great trigger, because coffee is a common drink to have during mornings and work breaks. Creating this association influenced more people to have them together.

Takeaway #3

Emotion

When it comes to making decisions, we are often more motivated by our emotions than our thoughts.

Marketers and salesman understand the power behind this concept and use emotions to get people to take action. We purchase things based on our emotions and use logic to rationalize the purchase.

This is nothing new, but Jonah dug a bit deeper.

His team of researchers analyzed every article in The New York Times for a few months and looked at which ones made it to the "most emailed" list. The discovery was that it didn't matter whether the emotions were positive or negative, but rather if they were high arousal or low arousal.

High arousal emotions are what get people to take the most action – on the positive side, it's things like awe, inspiration, excitement, and humor. On the negative side, it's emotions like anger, fear, and anxiety.

Low arousal emotions have the opposite effect. Relaxation and contentment may be positive, but they don't drive us to take action. Same with sadness and misery – they were found to not be that motivating.

When it comes to getting people to share your stuff, the higher arousal, the better.

Takeaway #4

Stories

Facts are necessary and can be persuasive, but if you can use those facts to form a coherent narrative, people are going to remember that information and spread it for you.

Stories are remarkable for making ideas popular. They are easy to remember, they tug at our emotions, and they are hidden with a lot of information that can influence our decisions.

If you tell someone 100 facts to support your idea, you may convince one person.

But if you tell them just one captivating story, you will leave a stronger impact, and they will be more likely to share your idea.

And there you have it. My four biggest takeaways from reading *Contagious* and how you can apply them to make your ideas get spread.

You Don't Find Your Passion, You Create It

TRYING TO "FIND your passion" implies that there is some purpose out there waiting for you, some higher calling, and all you have to do is discover it.

"Finding your passion" is a cliché excuse for not committing to anything.

You're not "destined" for anything – you can do whatever you want.

And usually, what you're most passionate about is right under your nose.

It's not about your passion, it's about your values.

If you are "looking for your passion" – switch your focus to your values.

You must understand what you value deepest in life, and pursue activities that help you maximize those values.

What kind of impact do you want to make on the world? What kind of skills would you like to develop? What do you want to create? What do you want to be good at?

You don't need to know these answers fully, but you do need to take action.

Once you get started, on anything, your mind mobilizes its forces to your aid.

But nothing happens until you start on something.

Passion is a side effect of mastery.

We tend to be excited and happy with things we're good at.

We tend to love things we're good at, especially when they impact people, or make us money.

You should adopt the mindset of a craftsman – shifting your focus away from "finding your passion" to instead mastering your craft.

On committing to become the best in the world at your thing.

Do this and amazing things will happen.

You may just discover your passion.

And remember...

Even the most passionate people in the world don't feel "passionate" all the time.

Like motivation, passion is an emotion. Which means it's inconsistent and unreliable.

So, instead of wasting energy "finding your passion" the lesson today is: pursue whatever interests you.

Get really good at your "thing."

And get started on something, anything.

Richard Branson's Success Secret

WE ALL HAVE 24 hours in the day.

Our results in life are determined by how we spend those hours.

And our energy determines exactly what we get out of those hours.

The difference between winners and losers is apparent in where they focus their energy.

Our energy is what controls how we spend our time.

And focusing your energy on the right things is the key to massive success.

You need to focus on the things you're good at, the things you love, and the things that are most important to you and your growth.

Energy comes from enthusiasm.

You cannot spend all day doing something you hate. But you can spend all day doing something you love.

So let's talk a bit about energy.

I think about it like money.

You only have a finite amount of energy and willpower each day.

From the time you wake up, to the time you go to sleep, you must spend and invest your energy wisely.

You cannot give your energy to lesser tasks if you want to do something big.

You must learn to delegate, outsource, and just plan avoid the things that are robbing you from your big vision.

Now, of course, there are ways to increase your energy.

Eating healthy, drinking lots of water, getting great sleep, stimulating the brain, and working out is the short list.

You see, many high energy professionals work pretty much all day.

And they all experience this "afternoon slump" – usually around 3pm.

It's normal – your brain needs a break from a heavy mental workload.

This is a good time to exercise and take a "productive break".

Usually, when you return to work after a productive break, you will find yourself full of energy and fresh ideas.

In fact, I've found some of the solutions to my most challenging problems have come when I step away from the computer, and go for a hike.

You'll see this common amongst most high performers – they all have a love for exercise and productivity.

Be An Activator

THERE ARE ONLY two types of people in this world.

Those that are passive.

And those that are active.

Most people fall into the passive category. They only do what they are asked. They await instructions, and require management.

Then there are those who are active are successful.

Successful people don't just do the job, but they do it right, and complete. And they certainty don't wait around for instructions or permission.

The one trait that separates successful people from those that aren't is this: the ability to initiate.

We refer to them here as activators.

They understand that life does not come to them; they are proactive and don't wait around for things.

Successful people are always on the offense and rarely on the defense.

They create their life, and shape their destiny, instead of merely going through life reacting.

Successful people understand the power of risk.

After all, initiating anything involves risk.

You're putting yourself out there, and there is most certainly a chance for failure.

But if you're only doing what you're told, avoiding risk and responsibility, then you're playing it safe.

Successful people take risks to become successful.

Because if great things didn't involve risk, more people would do them.

Tell me, in your life, are you an initiator? Or do you wait for instructions, permission, or "the perfect time"?

And what are the consequences of this to your dreams and goals? What are you missing out on?

SECTION III: PURPOSE

What's Your Purpose?

I'M GOING TO make an argument. See if it resonates with you or not.

Ready?

Your life's purpose is not about you. It's about serving others.

Your calling in this world is to help other people.

You have a specific voice and a unique set of experiences that you can use to help those in need.

The problem is that this truth terrifies most people. They don't want the responsibility or difficulty that comes with it. Most people want to go through life with their heads down, have some good times (or complain a lot), grow old, and die.

And that's perfectly fine. But if you're like me, you know there's more.

You have that burning up inside and you cant stand to play small.

You know your life's purpose is about leaving an impact on this world.

So how do you find out what that impact is exactly?

You might start reading a few books and blogs hoping to find the answer, but the truth is, the answer is inside of you.

Usually the thing you fear most is the thing you most need to do. Embrace that feeling and understand it's not something you're doing for yourself, but something you're doing for others.

You might think you're not important enough to have an impact, but real impact often starts with just one person.

And to help that one person, you need to push through your own fears and stick to your commitment to serve your fellow humans.

You don't need all of the answers, but getting started on this path will help you uncover some of these answers.

However, getting started on this path requires you to listen. Listen to yourself, to your heart, to your intuition, and to the signs the Universe is sending you.

Your heart is a great guide for determining which path to take.

Usually, though, your mind is trying to make logical decisions that are in direct opposition to your heart.

And most of the time we tend to listen to our minds and end up taking a safer, less fulfilling route instead of following our heart to our true desire and calling.

There are ways to listen to your heart without neglecting the rationale of your brain – and you'll learn those in the coming lessons.

For now, pay attention to the skills and abilities that come easier to you than others.

For example, I am a terrible public speaker, but I am excellent at sharing my thoughts and ideas through writing. That's why I wrote this book, and write for myself and select clients for a living.

The following points can summarize this lesson:

* Stay true to yourself

* Listen to your heart

* Pay attention to your experiences

* Take notice of your natural skills

* Serve others

Accept and understand what you find, and move forward from there.

What Is Success Anyway?

THIS IS A billion-dollar question.

Is success a number or some sort of unreachable destination?

Is an executive making $350k/year successful if he hates his job (and life)?

What about the writer who barely makes any money but is incredibly fulfilled? Does the lack of money make him unsuccessful?

Traditionally, success has been defined by money, fame, and power. We consider people successful based on the amount of money they make, their job title, or their shiny possessions (which may or may not have been purchased on credit).

But is this really the case?

About two years ago, I was grinding away as a door to door

Solar Salesman in Southern California (incredibly lucrative industry, btw). I was making bank – more money than I ever had in my life. What I made in a month was more than what I made every 6 months prior to that. I bought myself awesome clothes, a new Mercedes, and a shiny new watch.

And the funny thing is…

Absolutely nothing changed.

I wasn't more confident. I wasn't happier. Sure I did a bit better with women, but that's a product of materialism, and I realized I was attracting the wrong people into my life.

This made me realize that the superficial definitions of success did not affect what really mattered: my self worth.

In the book *Drive*, Daniel Pink debunks the definition of traditional success.

He argues that people need to pursue three intrinsic elements for true fulfillment:

Autonomy – being self directed.

Mastery – excelling at something that matters.

Purpose – the desire to work on something much bigger than yourself.

Of course, money is an extremely important element too. Before focusing on the intrinsic, you should be earning enough money to cover your basic needs. Just enough money so that "money problems" are off the table.

Now you can focus on what really matters:

Knowledge…

Personal Growth…

Happiness…

Meaningful Relationships…

Health…

Knowing what success means to you is a very deep and personal question, and a question that is absolutely necessary for you to identify your dream life and pursue it.

Don't let societal norms and consumerism define that for you.

Some questions to ask yourself as you ponder this writing:

Why do you want to be successful?

What excites you?

What makes you feel fulfilled?

Remember, success is about self worth, not net worth.

Money definitely matters, but not as much as you would think...

No amount of money can make you confident, charming, or happy.

But it sure can help.

FACE YOUR FEARS BEFORE BREAKFAST

COLD THERAPY IN the morning is one of the best life-hacks I've ever adopted.

Every morning, I get up and automatically head to the shower. I put the temperature on "cold AF," and let the water run for a minute or so.

In this time, I can feel my brain trying so hard to keep me in the comfort zone of life. It's trying to rationalize all the reasons why I shouldn't step into this cold shower. About why going back to bed under the warm covers is a much better idea.

It takes serious willpower to ignore that inner voice.

Sometimes I might stare at the cold water running for upwards of five minutes, willing myself to take that first step towards the shower spray. Usually, I make my feet move — one foot in front of the other — in spite of my brain telling me "no."

And this is the perfect metaphor for life.

The first step is always the hardest, and you'll always have fears and doubts.

But once you act in spite of your fear and take that first step, you realize it's not that bad.

The act of pushing through your fears and leaving the comfort zone is a great way to start every morning. It reinforces your willpower and mental toughness.

Plus, plenty of studies out there show that cold therapy helps you beat depression, boost your testosterone, and relieves stress.

As soon as you step into the cold shower, the shock wakes you up better than coffee can. You feel your breathing change, your blood flow is improved, and you feel alive. The electrical impulses from your nerve endings hit your brain and trigger a heightened sense of alertness.

And that's how I like to start each day.

For me, taking a cold shower every morning is a commitment to facing my fears. Because when you start your day in freezing cold water, all of a sudden, the other 'fears' you have don't seem that bad at all.

NEED VALIDATION?

MOST PEOPLE ARE motivated by external factors like money, status, and material success.

I know I was for most of my life. You might be too

We spend most of our lives craving validation from the outside world. We want to be successful in their eyes.

But once you start to appear "successful" — either by purchasing that awesome new car, new house or finally getting that promotion — you realize how superficial the whole concept is.

Sure, you get a little sugar high, but that fades quickly, and then you realize that happiness doesn't come from things or status. Happiness can only come from pursuing meaningful goals driven by internal motivation.

Tons of super successful people with all the things in the world are miserable for this very reason.

When you're driven solely by external motivation, you forget about the present, lose patience, and are unable to enjoy the journey.

Sucks, right?

Your highest priority should be a craft you are internally motivated to learn, practice, and get better at. When you follow your internal motivation, goals are a way to measure your progress, not validate your ego.

When you follow your internal motivation and focus on your "one thing," you'll almost always win. This is because you'll have the vision and patience for the long road of learning, failing, learning some more, and persisting.

Living your life chasing external motivations leads to internal conflicts. It kills your creativity, and suppresses your urge to do the things that you love the most.

Why?

Just to validate ourselves in the eyes of others?

It's a bit silly if you think about it. But sadly, this is life for most.

The most important thing I've learned is that success can't be measured by things in the external world, but only by how you feel within. Once you figure out the inner stuff, the outside always follows. Fulfillment comes from purpose, and the freedom to immerse yourself in the things you love doing most.

If you're not sure what that thing is, the question to determine it is:

If I wasn't getting paid for this, would I still do it anyway?

Figure out what your 'one thing' is and spend most of your time on it.

That's the key to an unreal life.

CHANGE IS HARD

OUR BRAIN LIVES and dies in the comfort zone.

It continually works to maintain the status quo, to keep us "safe."

Thus, making lifestyle changes is hard. And it's easy to get discouraged when you try something new and fail to get the results you wish for.

But the reality is that just making the effort is progress and part of the process.

Making successful changes is never linear; it's a process filled with small tiny steps that bring you closer to the ultimate goal.

And even failure on the way to that goal is growth.

For example, if you decide to change your mindset and take a risk starting that business you dream about and that business fails in three years, you're not exactly back to where you started.

You now have a wealth of life and business experience that will ultimately aid you on the path to success.

While researching for this lesson, I came across a scientific model for making successful changes. Although the *Transtheoretical Model* was developed to help people overcome addiction, it can be applied to reaching any significant goal that involves a lifestyle change.

These are the five stages of change as described in The *Transtheoretical Model*:

Precontemplation:

In this stage, you're not aware that change is necessary or desired. This may be because prior attempts to change failed or it may be due to lack of insight or awareness that problem exists.

To move past this stage, you need to become aware that there is a problem in your life, and that change is required to accomplish a goal or fulfill an aspiration. This can happen on its own, over time, or through others pushing you to make a change.

Contemplation

In this stage, you're aware that a change is needed in your

life, but you haven't made the commitment yet to actually change.

Here, you realize that something in your life is causing unwanted consequences, but you are still deciding if making a change will be worth it.

You're basically "on the fence."

Some people stay in this stage forever, never making a commitment to improve life.

One of the best ways to move past this stage is to make a list of the pros and cons related to making the change. Then, examine the negatives and think about how to overcome them. Or think about the "worst case scenario."

Usually, it's never as bad as your brain makes it out to be.

Preparation

This is when you start making plans to change.

You may start to do research on exactly what you need to do to be successful at your attempt to change, and you may start taking baby steps.

It's important to be realistic with your plans and making sure they are achievable.

Action

Now you're prepared and ready to execute on your plan.

The biggest drawback here is overcoming the initial obstacles — aka what you're not used to.

To stay successful and consistent, you need actionable strategies and external reinforcement, aka social support.

My best strategies include going to a conference filled with like-minded people, taking care of my brain and body, and reading motivational and positive stuff.

For social support, I look to a mastermind group of like-minded people to constantly support me, push me, and call me out on my bullshit.

Maintenance

After the first few months of making changes, things start to feel much easier. They're never as bad as you expect them to be.

Now, your new behaviors are more stable and consistent, and it's on you to celebrate your small success.

Here, you want to acknowledge your success and how much better things are now.

Relapses and regressions — going back to *"the old you"* — is normal and part of the process. Most attempts at change fail not because of a lack of progress, but because of a lack of maintenance.

That's why it's important to constantly avoid "bad stimulus" (i.e. your old temptations) and be around positive like-minded people, who help support the new you.

While making changes is always hard, it's much better to take action and push through rather than dream about the changes. After all, you could be dreaming about changes for your whole life.

The major factors that contribute to successful change are just like the factors that lead to success in all aspects of life: patience, persistence, and a strong commitment to continuous improvement.

Here are the biggest factors that will lead to your success:

1. Your desire to change is self-motivated.
2. Your change is rooted in positive thinking (not fear or guilt).
3. Your goal is specific and realistic.

But the most important factor is spending time with others who are role models for the change you're trying to make.

Failure Is Awesome

IF YOU'RE WAITING around for motivation to strike, or the "perfect time" to get started on changing your life, I have some bad news.

There is no such thing as the "perfect time," and as for motivation, the best way to get motivated is to take action.

We all have goals and ambitions, at least on some level. We're all driven to be better; it's in our nature.

But having goals and ambition can only take you so far.

Persistence and action taking – even when *you don't feel like it* – is the trait that separates the winners from the losers.

This is what the winning formula looks like:

Thoughts ->Actions ->Habits -> Success

Looking back on my year, I realize I haven't reached the goals I set for myself, and I'm about to tell you why. But before we start talking about what you need to achieve a goal, I want to drop a quick note about failure.

Failure is awesome.

Once you eliminate the fear of failure, well, you can do just about anything.

The problem is that we're more afraid to lose than we are to gain. That is what keeps us stuck. That is what keeps us from doing worthy things – like asking someone out on a date, executing on a business idea, or finally publishing that book.

But the reality is…

What we fear doing is usually what we most need to do.

Failure is feedback and the only true way to achieve growth.

If you ask any successful person for advice, they'll usually tell you to "go for it" or "just do it" and not be held back by the paralyzing fear of failure.

The first step is to define your fear and imagine the worst-case scenario that comes out of it.

Not so bad, right?

Remember, you miss 100% of the shots you don't take. The

only thing stopping you from achieving a goal is YOU.

Only YOU can overcome that self-doubting little voice in your head

So, ask yourself:

What are you going to do to make things happen, build momentum, and really start moving towards your goals?

Winners will start right now.

Balance Is Everything

WE SEE UNBALANCED lives all the time.

We see it in the dad who is always in the office and never with his family.

We see it in our friend who disappeared as soon as he got a girlfriend.

And with the friend who loves to have so much fun that he blew some major opportunities and messed up his career.

Balance is what allows you to perform at your highest ability, achieve clarity, define what you want out of life, and really get after it.

Having a more balanced life should be a goal on its own, and this lesson will show you a simple way of making progress on that front.

So with that, here are the main domains that affect your life and happiness:

1. Personal Development
2. Career
3. Health
4. Family
5. Relationships

I didn't mention financials. You can file that under career.

These five things are the most important aspects of your life and the things that contribute to your happiness and sense of well-being.

Your first step is to run an honest assessment about how you feel — and what you hope to achieve — for each one.

If your goals seem way out of reach, simply break them down into realistic goals that are achievable and contribute to the overall "bigger goal."

Once you have this assessment, it's time to set some objectives!

On the first of each month, I open up my journal and reflect on each category. I write down what went well in each area, what didn't, and what I'm going to do to make sure it doesn't happen again the following month.

This has not only made me more self aware, but also more accountable to the promises I make myself. Keeping track of the balance helps me make small progress each month — progress that significantly alters the quality of my life and moves me toward my ultimate self.

Your vision for the future should guide every decision you make today.

Automate Your Life For More Energy

USING YOUR PRECIOUS energy on meaningless tasks and trivial decisions will ultimately leave you with less time and less money.

I'm talking about things like paying your bills, going grocery shopping, and even pointless administrative work tasks that can be done by someone else for $3 an hour on UpWork.com.

Here are three of my favorite ways to free up more time:

1. Eat the same foods more or less every day.

I pay someone to make all my lunches and dinners in advance.

In the mornings I have a super shake (coconut milk, chocolate whey, spinach, and a banana). And my lunches and dinners are prepared beforehand, ready for me to eat.

This frees up so much of the time I would normally spend

cooking or just thinking about where I want to eat (and then going there, etc).

I pay $100 a week for this (I supply the groceries; they do the work).

This saves me all of the money I would otherwise spend eating out, keeps me on a healthy plan that boosts my productivity, but most importantly, it frees up SO MUCH TIME and MENTAL ENERGY.

2. Wear the same stuff (more or less) every day.

There's a reason why people like Steve Jobs and Mark Zuckerberg wear the same thing every day (more or less).

It's about reducing your decision-making fatigue.

This frees up mental energy to focus on more important things. Plus, you can still look great, even while wearing the same things every day.

My go-to outfit is a black or white v-neck and jeans on most days.

I don't wear the same clothes every day – I alternate different jeans and different v necks – but "jeans and a v-neck" is pretty much an automatic decision that frees up precious mental energy (your brain is the sharpest in the first few hours upon waking).

Plus, the outfit is super versatile and simple.

In my experience, Zara has the best fitting v-necks out there (and also the best value)

3. Hire a cleaning lady (and clean up after yourself).

There are lots of articles out there that talk about how "mess causes stress" and "how clutter affects your brain"

Instead of letting a mess accumulate and then dedicating hours (or a day) to clean your entire place, you can learn the art of picking up after yourself.

It's nothing ground breaking — when you finish using a dish, you clean it immediately instead of 'filing for later.' This will keep your place pretty clean, but you'll want to "deep clean" at least once every two weeks.

I pay a cleaning lady $75 to come deep clean once every two weeks, and my place is almost always clean.

4. Automate your bills…

Seriously, who likes to pay bills?

Almost every type of service you're paying for has an automatic bill setting.

They're already taking your money, don't let them take your time too.

You can use an app like Mint.com to easily set budgets and review all of your finances in one place.

This is far superior to sitting on the dining room table, with a stack of bills and a frown.

5. Automate your groceries.

If you don't have an assistant that does your grocery shopping for you, you can get certain things delivered to you using Amazon Fresh.

The best part is that you can set this up automatically — enter your shopping list once, and choose how often you want the items to appear on your doorstep.

I'm a huge fan of Amazon, having just finished reading Jeff Bezo's biography, The Everything Store. He is a true innovator. Have you seen the Amazon Dash? Coolest thing ever IMO.

And lastly, make everything in your life harmonious.

I hit the gym in the morning and then go to my favorite cafe to work from. The cafe is in-between the gym and my home.

Set up your life so that you're not stuck in traffic all day.

MOVEMENT, NOT MEDITATION

IF YOU RELY on motivation or "being in the mood" to do something, you're doing your ambitions and goals a major disservice.

As soon as you take action, motivation follows. Motivation comes from movement, not meditation.

Can you relate?

You're waiting for inspiration to strike.

You're waiting for that "perfect mood" to do something.

If you're relying on that, you're probably making minimal, if any, progress towards your goals.

Winners know that they must take action every day – be it small or large. They know that once they commit to something , they need to work toward it, especially when *they don't feel like it.*

Relying on emotions like motivation to reach a goal is a recipe for failure. You must remove emotions from the equation and be a professional.

That means creating a schedule and sticking to it.

I see this everywhere. Many people call themselves writers-, but never write. They only dream about writing and wait for "inspiration."

They wait for that million-dollar idea to come to them, while the professionals are forcing themselves to write everyday. Usually on deadline, and most of the time *"when they don't feel like it."*

As soon as you take action toward a goal, your mind mobilizes all its forces to your aid.

So…

If you're sitting around waiting for motivation or inspiration, I hope this lesson will snap you out of that delusion.

Take action and the motivation will follow.

This builds momentum.

Start small.

Schedule time for your goal and stick to it.

Don't rely on your "moods."

See you at the top.

Tomorrow Is For Losers

WHEN WE THINK about setting big goals, we almost instantly doubt whether we can achieve them.

As soon as the initial excitement about the prospect of a better future fades, the internal voice kicks in and attempts to sabotage us before we even begin.

There are three ways you can respond to this:

1. You can say it's impossible and give up.

This is most people.

2. You can tell yourself you're not ready and procrastinate.

The most common form of procrastination is learning. You just go from article to article, book to book, podcast to podcast, and course to course — learning a ton, but never taking action. Chances are, you don't need any more information. You need execution.

Winners figure things out on the fly.

3. You can get started, set deadlines, and pursue your dreams.

Tomorrow is for losers.

Tomorrow always turns into next week, next month, next year. And ultimately, you reach the end of your life and on your deathbed, you ask yourself "what if…"

If something is important to you and you're tired of avoiding what you know is your higher calling, if you're not satisfied with how your life is, you should get started **right now**.

You should understand there is **never** a perfect time.

And you should know that you'll be able to figure things out and overcome any obstacle that comes your way.

But it's important that you do one simple thing:

Just start.

Go all in.

True growth happens outside of the comfort zone when retreat is impossible.

Head to the island and burn your boat.

You are now in a situation where you must overcome obstacles or go under.

Your energy levels rise appropriately.

When you are fully invested and responsible for the outcome, you stop wasting time.

You find a work ethic you never knew you had.

And not only that, you become happier and more creative as a result.

Everything you do in life suddenly becomes relevant to the goal you are after, and opportunities will emerge all around you.

Sure, you'll struggle like hell and face some tough times. Everyone who has achieved something great has.

But through this struggle, you will forge your character and discover abilities you never knew you had.

You need to trust in your ability to learn, overcome obstacles, and accomplish goals.

You need to believe in yourself, and have a genuine trust that things will work out.

When you put yourself on the line, when you're "all in,", you will be passionate about your mission.

And you'll gain the attention of those around you.

People are naturally drawn to those who act boldly, take risks, and move toward their vision.

Being the leader of your life will make you feel "in control" and will take your confidence to levels you've never felt before — which will help you make more ambitious moves.

You're no longer letting "life happen to you." You're taking control and making things happen.

But remember…

You must get started.

Now.

What Do You Want Out Of Life?

THIS IS THE million dollar question.

Without defining it, you live life without aim. You just go through the motions, live reactively, and "let life happen to you."

But when you do know exactly what you want out of life?

You're on a mission to go get it.

You wake up energized and live passionately.

You know that time is fleeting, and as each day passes, you're one day closer to your death bed.

Today's lesson was inspired by Steven Covey's classic book, 7 Habits Of Highly Effective People. It's filed under "must read," and I try to revisit it at least once per year.

In the book, the author recommends that whatever it is you're pursuing, you start with the end in mind.

157

He then takes you through the following exercise.

Imagine yourself going to the funeral of a loved one.

Picture yourself driving there.

Parking the car, and getting out.

Now as you walk inside, you notice the flowers and the soft organ music.

You see the faces of your friends and family, and you feel the shared sorrow of losing someone you loved.

Now, as you walk down to the front of the room and look down at the casket.

You find yourself staring at yourself.

You're lying there peacefully, eyes closed, with your hands folded across your chest.

This is your funeral.

And it's five years from today.

Now there are three people who are speaking about you and the life you lived.

What do you want these people to speak about?

What do you want to be known for?

How do you want to be remembered?

Answer these questions and use it to guide your decisions, today.

Keep in mind the end goal, and take small steps every day to reach that goal.

WHY YOU DON'T REACH YOUR GOALS

LET'S REFLECT ON the year.

Did you achieve the goals you set?

Did you do the things you said you would?

If you're like me — if you're like most — the answer is: probably not.

Most of us set big noble goals at one point or another, and listed out the things we'd like to achieve.

But most of the time, these things take a back seat to our daily motions, and vanish in the sands of time.

There are three main reasons for this:

No Accountability or Social Support.

This is extremely important for positive reinforcement, and most importantly, accountability to goals.

The truth is that being accountable to your friends and family is a recipe for failure (studies even prove it), and a lot of the time, your friends and family are secretly hoping for you to fail.

It's why joining a mastermind with likeminded people dedicated to growth has the ability to change your life.

No Willpower

Reaching big goals is hard. It takes sacrifice and delayed gratification.

The person that can delay gratification to reach a goal wins.

That's easier said than done, though, as short term rewards feel better than holding out for long term gain.

We must learn to understand and control our emotions and impulses.

No Clear Vision

This is the most important point.

Your vision is the driving force that makes you take action even when *you don't feel like it*. It's responsible for pushing through the hard times and overcoming any obstacles that come your way (spoiler alert: there will be a lot of obstacles).

The common problem with most people's visions is that they are incredibly vague and superficial.

Your vision for the future determines your reality.

It controls your beliefs, how you think, and what actions and decisions you make in the present.

Your vision will create a clearer path for your making decisions and living your life.

YOUR VISION

THIS LESSON WILL help you explore a few different ways to create a powerful vision that serves you, and how to use that vision to achieve your goals.

Your vision is where you want to be and your path for how you'll arrive.

This is personal, and only you can decide the ultimate vision for yourself.

It's important that you stay true, devoid of any validation or external expectations.

Your personal vision is all about YOU — living your ideal life and spending your time exactly how you want.

OK now that's out of the way, let's get into the actionables.

Take A Personality Test

I'm a big fan of the "Strengths Finder" test.

This will help you understand yourself better, which will help you to create a purpose and vision that is aligned with your own talents, personality traits, and values.

Create Your Five Year Plan

This exercise forces you to visualize your dream life, and the short time frame (5 years) makes everything realistic.

It's quite simple: what do you want your life to look like five years from now? Focus on your career, lifestyle, and relationships. Visualize in detail what you want it to look like.

Now, write down what you need to move you towards your vision.

When I sat down to do this, it changed my life forever.

Now, whenever I'm faced with a tough decision, it ultimately comes down to the question: does this serve my five year vision?

And now that you have the foundations in place, it's time to go deeper and ask yourself the following questions.

Are direction, purpose, and challenge signaled in this five year plan?

Am I aware of the strategies and skills that will help me accomplish what I've written?

And the most important question of them all:

Does this vision of the future inspire me to get out of bed each morning?

SIDE PROJECTS: DO THAT THING YOU'VE ALWAYS WANTED TO DO

THIS LESSON IS about side projects – those magical things that allow you to express and explore your creativity, build an additional income stream, and develop some unique skills in the process.

Side projects are the new resume.

My side projects ended up turning into my career.

You can see these examples everywhere.

Many comedians are scoring TV show appearances and lucrative deals after building followings on sites like Twitter or Vine.

Artists are getting record deals after going viral on YouTube.

And even authors are self-publishing their way to fame

with Amazon.

Not only do side projects lead to these lucrative situations, they bring more diverse ideas into your current work and help you avoid burnout by working on something you love.

When you're working on a side project, you're utilizing your intellectual curiosity, learning new skills, and are on a path for continuous improvement.

The most important thing is that you get started right now.

How?

First, write down a list of things you wished you were better at, or something you'd like to create.

Don't get caught up in the "how" (and analysis paralysis), just focus on identifying your desires first.

What do you want to create?

Pick something from the list, and take the first step right now.

Do something that will produce just enough momentum for you to move forward.

Now, the all too common excuse and barrier is time. And I get it, trust me. I have a full time job and juggle multiple side projects, including this book.

The first step you need to take is to remove non-essential stuff from your life. Track how you spend (or waste) your time.

Are you watching TV for two hours after work?

Playing on your phone for 30 minutes every morning?

Spending your lunch breaks gossiping at Chilis?

All of these can be replaced with "side hustle" time. And trust me, if you can find just 30-60 dedicated minutes to work on your side hustle each day, you're on a great path.

You can dedicate a set time in the morning, or in the evenings after work.

I prefer mornings, as that's when my creativity and willpower are at the highest level.

And if you're still thinking you don't have the time, go to bed earlier, and wake up earlier.

Remember – what we end up building, ends up building us.

SYSTEMS VS. GOALS

I ORIGINALLY LEARNED about this concept from Scott Adams, in his book *How To Fail at Almost Everything and Still Win Big.*

Goals are powerful things.

They're a reason for getting out of bed in the morning.

And as humans, growth and exploration, is one of our driving factors.

But here's the thing. When you set a goal and invest your emotions in the outcome, you are living in a state of nearly continuous failure until the goal is achieved.

Over time, that wears on your happiness, making you feel heavy and uncomfortable.

And when you achieve your goal, you celebrate and feel terrific. But then you realize you just lost the thing that gave you purpose and direction.

You can either feel empty and useless, or set new goals and enter the cycle of permanent pre-achievement failure.

I'm a big fan of the set a small goal, crush it, and set a bigger goal model. But to crush even the smallest of goals, you need a system. You CANNOT rely on your motivation or any emotions for that matter.

This concept of systems made me reevaluate the way I think about goals.

A system is a way for you to maintain your personal energy in the right direction, get constant feedback, and be able to monitor your progress.

For example...

Losing twenty pounds is a goal, but eating right is a system with a positive outcome.

Making a million dollars is a goal, but being a serial entrepreneur is a system.

Publishing a book is a goal, but writing each morning is a system.

If you do something every day — regardless of "how you feel" — it's a system.

If you're waiting to achieve it someday in the future, it's a goal.

The goal oriented people wake up with a feeling that they are in a race against time, and they must achieve their goal or they are a failure.

The systems people wake up and show up everyday, knowing that the system is bringing them closer and closer to their goal.

Usually, when you set out to achieve something, you end up with a completely different result — sometimes even better than the result we originally set out after.

Now, don't get me wrong. Setting goals is important and helps guide your every day actions. But it's more important to have a vision for the future and create systems to help get you there.

Being overly focused on one goal may work for some people, but for others, it may cause stress, anxiety, and discouragement.

How To Become An Overnight Success

ARE YOU EXACTLY where you want to be?

In life, in love, and in your career?

I'm assuming the answer is: absolutely not.

We live in an age of immediate gratification.

We want things, we want them fast, and we want them now.

And to make it even worse, we live in an age where everyone around us showcases only the best part of their lives like some kind of highlight reel. It's easy to compare ourselves to others and feel badly, but of course, they're leaving out the struggle, the long nights, and the unique journey that got them where they are.

And most are exaggerating or fabricating their online lives to appear more successful or happy.

We're living in the most technologically connected time in history, yet this may just be the period with the most discontent humans.

In the West, we have "everything," yet we are constantly searching for something.

Our minds are never at peace.

We are constantly comparing ourselves to others.

This lesson is to remind you that success is not linear, and everyone goes through a crazy, unique journey that ultimately takes them there.

This lesson is to remind you that your biggest assets in this game of life are patience, focus, and most importantly, consistency.

In this time of instant gratification and poor attention spans, the one who can have a long-term vision for his life, create a plan, and commit the necessary time over the long run to achieve results...

Wins the game.

Just remember:

"It takes fifteen years to become an overnight success."

FIVE OVERNIGHT SUCCESSES (THAT WEREN'T)

IN THE LAST lesson, we talked all about the age of immediate gratification.

I talked about the façade people put on, and why comparing yourself to everyone's social media "highlight reel" is causing anxiety, depression, and a feeling of "lack."

Today's lesson contains a few examples of "overnight successes" — that had accomplished next to nothing before the age of 30.

It's all too easy to see successful people and think they've always been this way. But success works in mysterious and random ways. It's almost never linear, or as we expect it.

So here goes...

Five overnight successes (that weren't).

#1 Jack Dorsey

Jack was an anti-social and punk-rock skater well into his mid-twenties.

His first company, a cab dispatching program, had slowly fizzled out and failed.

His next move was to approach Ev Williams, who was running Odeo, a podcasting company. He shared his vision for the idea of an instant messaging service.

They teamed up to pursue it full time. Jack was appointed the first CEO of Twitter.

He was 30 years old at the time.

(For more, I highly recommend reading the book "Hatching Twitter.")

#2 Tim Westergren

Tim started Pandora at the age of 35.

Prior, he was a failed musician who was working as a nanny to pay the bills.

As a new founder, Tim brought Pandora to near bankruptcy in the first two years.

Being 400k in debt, he somehow convinced 50 employees to work without pay for two years.

#3 Jan Koum

Jan was a dropout from San Jose State College.

He worked at Yahoo as an infrastructure engineer for nine years, then quit to go on a backpacking trip across South America.

Upon his return, he applied for a job at Facebook and was rejected.

On his 33rd birthday, he founded WhatsApp, which was later acquired by Facebook for $19 billion dollars.

#4 Peter Thiel

Peter Thiel graduated from Stanford Law in 1992 and landed a job at a prestigious Manhattan law firm.

After only seven months, Peter Thiel realized that being a lawyer was miserable work and went to work in the finance industry.

Three years later, at age 31, he founded PayPal.

Four years after founding the company, he was acquired by Yahoo for $1.5 Billion.

#5 Mark Cuban

At 28, Mark Cuban was living on the floor of a three-bedroom shared apartment.

He graduated from college at 24, and immediately started working as a bartender in Dallas.

His first "real job" saw him selling computers for $18,000 a year, but he was fired for going against his boss.

At 25, he started a software consulting company called MicroSolutions. Seven years later, at 32, Cuban sold this company and netted $6 million dollars.

The rest is history.

And there you have it.

Five extremely successful people who hadn't accomplished much before thirty.

I know reading these stories inspires me, instills a feeling of "ahhhh it's all good," and reminds me that I'm on the path.

Remember, life and success work in mysterious ways.

If You're Not Learning, You're Dying

IF YOU'RE NOT learning, you're dying.

Literally.

Your brain cells stop growing.

To live a successful and happy life, it's extremely important to nurture the brain and give it what it needs daily.

Here are a few things that literally make your brain grow:

Having sex...

Running...

And of course, reading — reading things that inspire you, expose you to new ideas, and give you an advantage in your industry.

It's been said that "all leaders are readers," and I completely agree with that. I haven't met one truly successful person out there who doesn't read.

For example, Warren Buffet spends 5 to 6 hours each day reading books, newspapers, and corporate reports.

Bill Gates reportedly reads 50 books per year (almost one per week).

Mark Zuckerberg reads at least one book every two weeks.

Elon Musk grew up reading two books per day, according to his brother.

And even Oprah Winfrey credits reading to her massive success. I think she said something like: "Books were my pass to personal freedom".

Reading a good book is like borrowing the brain of the author. You get to absorb all of their life experiences, and learn from them.

The benefits of daily learning are tremendous and invaluable.

All it takes is one idea in one book to completely change the trajectory of your life.
If you look to the most successful people in the world, you'll see that they consistently invested in their learning and uninterrupted self reflection.

Taking time to learn and reflect helps you understand the world around you.

It helps you gain clarity, see problems before they arise, have creative breakthroughs, and understand exactly what you want from this life, and what you want to contribute.

Today, it's all too easy to get sucked into the illusion of productivity, when in fact, "productivity" is just another form of procrastination.

Keeping yourself busy with meaningless "busy work", in order to avoid the real, uncomfortable internal and external work necessary to move forward in your life.

Are You In The Zone?

IF YOU DO what you've always done, you'll get what you've always gotten.

Today's lesson is not about bashing the comfort zone — where people go to die — but instead, to introduce you to a new zone that we should all strive towards:

The Zone Of Proximal Development.

The concept was developed by Lev Vygotsky, a Russian developmental psychologist who died nearly 100 years ago.

The idea is this: Everything you want to do exists on a spectrum ranging from incredibly easy to impossibly difficult.

And somewhere on that spectrum exists the upper limit of what you're capable of doing on your own.

And just beyond those limits, is your zone of Proximal Development, where you'll find the tasks that you can perform with extra effort, and proper support and instruction (ah, the power of community).

Entering this zone is not comfortable or easy.

In fact, most people live their entire lives without even daring to enter this zone.

But it's where we go to expand our abilities and create the possibility of achieving our dreams.

A zone where vision, impact, and creating an amazing life drives all of our moves.

A powerful question to ask yourself:

What's the one thing you know you need to do, but is way beyond your comfort zone?

THINK LIKE A BOSS

WHETHER YOU RUN a million-dollar company or a small internet side hustle, you must project the image of a confident and competent leader to the world.

However, self-assurance doesn't come naturally for many.

But learning the art of confidence will help you find composure, no matter the situation.

In the book *Think Confident, Be Confident*, Marci G. Fox defines confidence as:

"Knowing that you can walk into any situation with the skills, strengths, and abilities you need.... You know that you can deal with the situation, or find someone or something to help you"

This is the most powerful way of thinking, and I remind myself of this every morning.

Self-doubt prevents you from taking the risks necessary to

achieve anything.

It prevents you from launching a new business...

Stops you from asking for a raise…

Asking that attractive stranger out on a date…

Self-doubt is when you overestimate the risk in your mind. When you forget how capable and competent you are, and instead see yourself as vulnerable.

Most of the time, self-doubts come from things that have gone wrong in the past, or anxiety about the future.

Confidence allows you to focus on the present , on exactly what is happening now.

Kill Your Negative Thoughts and Stick To The Facts

Just one negative thought can lead to a snowball effect of more negativity. It's much better to focus on the positive.

Negative thoughts are normal. A mentor taught me to think of them as a speeding car on a freeway. Let it pass. Don't obsess and let one thought lead to a tangent of negative "what if's" and a highlight reel of your previous failures.

Self-doubt and anxiety are merely emotions that can be

controlled.

Anytime I have a negative self-limiting thought, I ask myself – what evidence do I have that makes this true?

If I find out that in fact, it's a valid self-limiting belief, then I start to brainstorm creative solutions to overcome the problem.

Usually it involves learning a new skill, or delegating to someone else.

Acknowledge ALL of your accomplishments.

It's so easy to get caught up with all the bad things that have happened to us, that we forget all the good in our life...

You must always keep track of, and express gratitude for all of your successes – no matter how small and big.

This does wonders for your confidence and happiness.

At the end of each day, write down everything you've completed, learned, or accomplished.

Always take credit, and relish in your successes – no matter how small.

SECTION IV: SUCCESS

MONEY OR PASSION?

THIS IS A controversial one.

Many people are saying "follow your passion" and the money will follow.

I disagree with these people.

It often, unfortunately, doesn't work that way.

Especially when you run these passion-based businesses like a hobby and not a real business – you know, with strategy and a plan.

Many of these "follow your passion" types subscribe to the old "build it and they will come model." And in my opinion, they are in for a rude awakening.

So many of these "passionate" entrepreneurs are BROKE.

Why?

They don't understand marketing and sales – the key driver of any business.

There are so many amazingly passionate entrepreneurs with great products and services. But without the right plan, they have nothing.

This lesson will help you make sure that doesn't happen to you.

Now, I'm all about passion. I think you should follow it – for yourself, and to share your unique message and gift with the world.

But that doesn't necessarily mean it will turn into a profitable business.

You should definitely pursue your passion, but don't quit your day job until your 'passion' is showing you signs that it can and will be a profitable business.

So how do you know if your passion can be a profitable business?

First, identify your passion and then your offer.

What are you selling? What kind of value do you provide in exchange for people's hard-earned money?

From there, research the market. A simple Google search

will work wonders. See what businesses are out there based around your passion and how those businesses are packaging and selling your offer. Use SimilarWeb for more advanced research

Here's a big tip:

Your passion can most likely be a profitable business if it helps solve a problem for people.

If your passion is not based on solving a problem for people and is just something "cool," you may be able to build an audience or entertain people. But those likes and popularity won't necessarily translate into sales and revenue – the key driver behind business.

So, you've done your basic research and see that your passion is indeed able to solve a problem and provide a solution in a profitable marketplace.

Don't quit your day job just yet!

You need strategy and a specific plan, with measurable goals, and projections in mind. If you go into business with just your passion and your motivation to change the world, you're destined to go broke.

PLANNING IS PROCRASTINATION

LET'S TALK ABOUT your big idea.

I'm assuming you have one (or many).

You set out to figure out how to do it, how everything would work. And then you rationalized that you couldn't do it, so you move on to the next big idea.

And this cycle continues.

Can you relate?

I certainly can. More times than I can count.

What happens here is dangerous. Your brain scrambles and jumps into the mechanisms of implementation.

You get overwhelmed by the details, the "how," before you can even make a commitment to your idea.

Your uninformed optimism quickly turns into informed

pessimism.

And sure, it seems logical to try to figure out exactly how everything is going to work before we commit to something. However, this turns into a million little details that overwhelm us and prevent us from even starting.

Successful people go in on an idea and commit to learning and figuring out everything on the fly. And they most certainly are ready to pivot, based on feedback from the market and the Universe.

So next time you have that big idea, instead of jumping into the details or "the how," first understand the why behind it.

Why this idea? Why do you want to do it?

(Highly recommended learning on the subject: *Start With Why* by Simon Senek.)

When you understand your why, you have a driving force that will help you push through all obstacles and challenges.

When you have your why clearly defined, you'll know if you should move on or commit to the idea.

If it's a maybe, then just file it into your "notebook of big ideas" and refer back to it at least once per year.

When you know your why, then you can move onto your how.

How everything will work and how you'll make it happen.

Now, if the idea is really big, like change-the-world Uber style big, don't think beyond the first 12 months.

Think about the first steps you need to take to get things up and running, and to take that big idea out of your head.

And into the world.

It doesn't have to be perfect, nor does it have to be good. All that matters is that it's out in the world and it's tangible. Improvements come later, but you'll want validation on your idea first.

You'll find out that once you execute and put your idea out into the world, you build momentum, and more and more "serendipitous opportunities" start appearing out of nowhere.

Just remember: everyone has big ideas, but few people execute on them.
Most dive into the details, develop an attitude of informed pessimism, and never even get started.

But when you focus on today's work — not tomorrow's — your ideas will become a reality.

Procrastinate Much?

LET'S TALK ABOUT analysis paralysis.

The phrase is defined as *the state of over-analyzing (or over thinking) a situation so that a decision or action is never taken, in effect paralyzing the outcome.*

Here's an example.

A friend emailed me to tell me about ALL of the books and blogs he was reading, the courses he took, and even more he had planned to take to "get ready to launch."

Then and only then, would he be ready to START testing his business idea.

Hold up, dude....

You're going to do ALL OF THAT, before you even know that the market wants your idea?

No, no, no....

Money belongs to those who take action. Overanalyzing will prevent you from doing anything.

Are you trying to be perfect? Waiting for the perfect time?

You'll get started after you finish a few books on the subject, take a few more courses, or (insert your excuse here)?

Or are you just procrastinating because you're afraid of the prospect of failure?

As an entrepreneur, you should strive for failure. It's the most valuable learning lesson you could hope to receive.

And it happens a lot more quickly than waiting for the perfect time, or "learning as much as you can."

Hell, I'm convinced that successful people are just people who failed more often than the rest of us.

And if you haven't failed in anything recently, you're definitely not living up to your potential.

Here's the truth about making money: you need to take bold action (like how Richard Branson launched Virgin with just $200 and no prior experience).

You don't need all the information in the world.

In fact, I'll recommend you go on an information diet and focus on what really matters to you and your business.

You need to get really clear on your intentions and get good at 1 or 2 things.

You need to follow 1 or 2 trusted sources.

And most importantly, you need to avoid shiny object syndrome and stay the motherfucking course.

Four Step System For How To Reach Your Goals

WE ALL HAVE goals, ambition and motivations – at least on some level.

We're all driven to be better. It's in our human nature.

But ambition and motivation can only take you so far.

Most of us approach goal setting like a wish-list.

A goal is **not** a "nice to have."

It's something you ACHIEVE (that means, it requires persistent hustle).

Most won't ever dedicate the time to think and create a realistic PLAN.

And this is why, come February, most of the "motivated" New Years Resolutioners have **FAILED MISERABLY.**

You cannot rely solely on motivation to reach your goals.

You need to plan.

The more detailed your plan is, the better your chances of success.

A good plan is **measurable**.

You track metrics that keep you **accountable.**

And about that big, audacious goal you're about to aggressively tackle (good job btw, dude)?

The end-goal should be broken down into **smaller goals.**

Achievable ones.

It shouldn't feel like a never-ending struggle (even though it is at times).

You should stop and celebrate small wins.

Went to the gym 3 times last week? HELL YAS.

Wrote 10 pages of that book you've been meaning to write? AWW YEE.

ANY PROGRESS IS SUCCESS (and should be treated

that way).

To Achieve A Goal You've Never Achieved Before, You Need Four Things:

#1 Planning And Preparation

You can't just wing it and expect great things to happen. You need a well-defined and structured plan. This plan should be realistic and fit in with your life and personality.

#2 Accountability And Social Support

Telling people what we want to achieve is the first step. Talking about your goals with anyone breathes life into it, especially when you surround yourself with like-minded people who want to see you succeed.

Studies show that accountability to a professional, like a coach, is more valuable than accountability to a friend or family member.

#3 Incentive

You have to understand **why** you are setting this goal.

The why is your mission to the end result. You have to really dig deep to figure this out, and once you do, constantly remind yourself of the end result you're seeking. The more specific you can be, the better.

For example, finishing this book before the end of the month is my goal. And to celebrate that goal, I'm going to take a motorcycle trip through Patagonia.

Deadline

There's this thing called the law of diminishing intent.

The more time that passes after you set a goal, the less likely you are to make it happen.

This is why it's wise to set deadlines.

Deadlines propel action. Period.

The further away a deadline, the more likely we are to procrastinate, which is why it's smart to break down any "big goal" into a set of mini goals with realistic and close deadlines.

Regardless, achieving a goal, no matter how small, propels us with the momentum needed to take on even bigger goals.

The cycle looks something like this:

Goal Setting -> Planning -> Deadline -> Commitment -> Discipline -> Accomplishment -> Satisfaction -> Bigger Goal -> Repeat

How To Start An Online Business From Scratch

NOW THAT YOU know a bit about analysis paralysis and how it can prevent you from getting started, I want to tell you about another limiting belief that will prevent you from succeeding as an entrepreneur, and well, everything else in your life.

It's the belief that you you're not ready "yet" for _____ (insert whatever excuse you have here).

I'll repeat this from the last lesson: there will never be a perfect time to get started.

If you don't understand that, stop reading here, and come back when you "get it."

But if you do get it…

Let's talk about:

How To Get Your Business Idea Up And Running Online ASAP

The first thing you want to do is get crystal clear on your business idea and your why behind it.

Not "why" you want to do it (even though having a sense of "mission" is absolutely important). But WHY someone else should trade his or her hard earned money for what you offer.

And once you understand that, you need to get crystal clear on WHO that person is (and more importantly - why they need what you're offering).

In your marketing, you should never want to appear "everything to everyone." You'll connect with no one.

In today's rapidly connected online world, you only need to connect with a very small amount of people to grow a successful business.

So don't be afraid to be as authentic as possible. Unless you're a terrible person. Then disregard that advice (see: 1,000 true fans).

Now, once you understand your value proposition (what you offer in exchange for money), and you have your customer avatar (who wants/needs your offer), the fun begins.

The first thing I would recommend is competitive research.

Nothing fancy or complicated here. Google your offer and see who your top competitors are.

See how they're selling (use similarweb to see where they are selling, too).

And watch them closely.

If you are seeing a lot of competitors, this is a great thing. It means there is a lot of money going around in whatever it is you're trying to do.

Don't be "scared" by competition. It's healthy, gives you a perfect model of exactly what's working, and makes it easier to be better than your competitors (by watching them closely and seeing how you can improve on the idea).

And if you can't find any competitors, there's a pretty good chance that there isn't much money going around in that space.

Unless it's so absolutely game changing that you're the first to market (and if that's the case, I'd start pitching for venture capital, because trying to sell new product categories is no easy feat for a first time entrepreneur).

Once you understand your offer, build your customer avatar,

and get a grasp on your competitors, you're now ready to test your offer in the market.

We'll dive into all of that in detail in the next lesson.

Your Actionable Business Plan

THE LAST TWO lessons were meant to help you with the "mindset" of business. And now, I'm going to show you how to put everything into action.

You need to understand that it's easier than ever to validate your business idea quickly and cheaply.

But you must be crystal clear on the following:

1. What your offer is and why people need it
2. Who your target market is
3. What your competitors are up to

Before we dive in to this valuable lesson, get your mind right. Relieve yourself of any weird performance anxiety and think of this as a simple test. You'll produce better work in a looser mood, anyway.

Your mindset here should be that of someone collecting data and feedback from the market. Data that will help you understand your business more than any book or course will.

And if you get your first few customers from this test, congratulations, you have yourself a real business.

It's not easy, but very simple.

So let's begin:

#1: Know your Target Market and WHY they need your offer.

#2: Target them by interests on Facebook and run different variations of advertisements to them. Test different messages, appeals, and offers.

#3 Send them to a landing page that simply asks for their email in exchange for a free version of what you're offering. This is called a lead magnet, and I'll expand on this in a minute.

#4 Begin the sales conversation. Get to know them. Build what marketers call "know, like, and trust." Find out how to serve them and deliver.

If nobody is clicking on your advertisements, you need to work on your ad copy, offer, or targeting.

If people are clicking, but not entering their email, you need to work on your landing page copy or offer.

If people are clicking and entering their email, but not being responsive to your emails, you need to work on your emails.

Simple, right?

The best part is that today there are tons of tools that do ALL OF THIS for us (and most of them offer free trials). No need for designers, coders, webmasters, advertisers, or statisticians.

Now, before I put all of this stuff into actionable terms and provide you with the tools and resources you need., I'd like to tell you the #1 mistake I see new people make in business.

They're painfully boring and afraid to stand out.

They try to be everything to everyone. And in turn, they connect with no one.

My #1 piece of advice is to be as specific as possible with your offer and targeting.

For example, when I said "Hey, I'm Alon, and I'm an Online Marketing Consultant," I had no business.

But when I started saying "Hey, are you a best-selling author that wants to deliver massive value to your email list to increase loyalty and sales?"

... I ended up with more business than I could handle.

Okay, side tangent over.

Let's get into the actionable bits:

#1 Know Your Target Market

I've linked to a "conversion questionnaire" at the end of this book – fill it out and your lead magnet and advertisements will pretty much write themselves.

#2 Create a Lead Magnet

This is how you get people to know you, like you, trust you, and eventually do business with you.

Your lead magnet is meant to build your credibility and allow people to trust you to solve their problems. It should be valuable and help people for free.

A lead magnet can be anything. The most popular seem to be free reports that solve a problem for your target market.

You can write it out in Microsoft Word and find someone on Fiverr to make it look pretty for $5.

#2 Test Multiple Facebook Advertisements

Use a tool called AdEspresso (free 14 day trial) to advertise your free lead magnet and send traffic to a landing page.

This tool allows you to test multiple variations of ads.

The most important element to test is the image, but also test your ad copy. You can easily create a ton of different variations with this tool. You get all kinds of data back from them – what ads are working, what targeting interests are most relevant to your offer, and way more.

And the best part is that you can get this meaningful data for as little as $5 a day on ads!

#3 Send Facebook Ads To Your Landing Page

Use ClickFunnels to easily build a landing page with no design or coding experience required (free trial).

A landing page is a simple page that collects an email address in exchange for your lead magnet.

My tip is to keep it as simple as possible.

Within the software, you can "split test" your landing page – which means your traffic will automatically get diverted to 1 of 2 (or more) variations of the page. This will help you understand exactly what's working for you.

With testing, I wouldn't worry too much about design or small details – test different offers or headlines.

It's easy to get lost in testing. Always focus on one variable at a time, choose a winner, and then test new things.

#4 Begin The Sales Conversation

Sign up for Mailchimp, a free and easy email marketing software.

Don't caught up in analysis paralysis with advanced email marketing, auto-responders, and complex sales funnels. For now, focus on understanding your potential customer and solving their problems for them.

I'd recommend setting up one email to automatically go out to someone once they enter their email on your landing page. Use this opportunity to better understand your potential customer by simply asking what they are struggling with, or offer a free call where you'll help them (don't talk about yourself too much or try to sell them here).

Once you understand your prospect, you can expand on your marketing and start solving their most painful problems — the problems that they'll gladly pay money to resolve.

Now, by no means is this a magic formula for success.

But it's a damn quick and easy way to understand where your offer stands in the market, and to begin creating relationships with your potential customers.

That's it.

No need for analysis paralysis.

This lesson is all you need to get started.

Remember – DONE is better than NONE.

Go get some feedback from the market.

BECOME SO GOOD THEY CAN'T IGNORE YOU

THE OTHER DAY I was reading Steve Martin's memoir, *Born Standing Up*. And while he breaks down the formula for achieving world-class success in the entertainment industry, I feel the message can be applied to anyone.

The big message from the book can be broken down into one big idea: ignore the frustration, comparing yourself to others, and looking for "short cuts."

Instead, focus on becoming good. Really damn good.

When you focus exclusively on that, recognition and success will come so fast that it might just overwhelm you.

Here are two more big ideas I got from the book:

Big Idea #1 Understand and then Innovate.

Putting in the time isn't enough. Grinding isn't enough.

You must understand and innovate.

Steve wasn't just memorizing punch-lines for standup comedy, he was figuring out the essence of what made things "funny."

He then used these insights to move past the punch-line formula that everyone was using in comedy at the time.

Without this understand and innovation, Steve would have just been "another good comedian" instead of the legend he is now.

Big Idea #2 Stay Focused.

Steve Martin is quick to clarify that working hard over a long period of time was not the key to his success.

He constantly fought the urge to start working on other projects, jumping into "exciting opportunities," and looking for shortcuts.

Martin makes it extremely clear with this quote:

"If you don't saturate your life in a single quest, you'll dilute your focus to a point where becoming outstanding becomes out of reach."

His three-step system for success is quite simple:

1. Understand

2. Innovate

3. Stay Focused

If you're looking to become world-class in whatever it is that you're doing, there is only one thing you need to focus on: becoming so good they can't ignore you.

CREATE A SUCCESS SYSTEM

IF YOU'RE RELYING solely on your motivation to reach a goal, you're in for a rude awakening.

Sure motivation helps, especially with getting started, taking initial action, and building emotion.

But motivation is an emotion.

It doesn't last forever.

And any meaningful goal takes a long time to achieve.

If you rely solely on your motivation, you'll get burned out before you reach your goal. What's far more important than motivation, is shaping your environment and habits to aid your success.

It's normal for us to believe all of our habits are a product of motivation, talent, and effort.

And don't get me wrong, those things definitely matter.

The thing is, over time, especially a long period of time, your motivation and even your will power tend to get overpowered by distractions, procrastination, unconscious fears, bad habits, fake busywork, and reactive behavior. That's why it's extremely important, if you want to reach your highest potential, to develop systems that protect you from your lower self.

For example, I find that in the morning on an empty stomach is when I can do my best writing. So I created a winning morning routine and don't open any distracting social media or even my emails until my writing is done for the day.

This is usually 2-3 uninterrupted hours in the morning — just me, my coffee, and a blank Word document.

I literally don't allow myself to eat until the writing is complete. A delicious breakfast is my reward and really forces me to write, even when I don't feel like it.

This system has created a habit, which means, my work gets done, regardless of motivation.

Here are three ways to develop successful environment systems:

Automate Good Decisions

Design an environment that automatically makes good decisions for you.

For example, buying smaller plates can help you lose weight by automatically setting your portion size. A study from Cornell showed that people eat 22% less food by switching from a 12 inch to a 6 inch plate.

For productivity, plan your day out in the evening, follow a morning routine, and execute your most important tasks first thing in the morning before allowing the interruptions of the day to take hold.

Use software like SelfControl or Freedom to block out social media sites and kill your procrastination.

Design Habits That Support Your Current Patterns

You'll want to create an environment where good habits are "in the way" of your normal behaviors.

For example, you are more likely to go to the gym if it's part of your commute. You can plan to go to the gym either before work, or after work on your way home.

Kill The Negative Influences

Get rid of things that distract you from your goals.

If you're trying to get in shape, keep junk food out of your house.

If you're trying to get things done, block out social media, and find a dedicated and uninterrupted workspace.

Understand Yourself and Your Patterns

Like all advice here, everything is completely subjective.

What works best all depends on you.

And it all starts with getting clarity into yourself.

For example, I work best early in the morning, after a solid night of sleep and fresh cup of coffee.

Others swear that they work best late into the night.

It's all a personal preference and takes a bit of experimentation to find out what works for you.

CREATE THE RECIPE, NEVER DO THE COOKING

THAT WAS MY biggest "a-ha" moment as an entrepreneur.

It's the secret all millionaires know.

Work to create assets, don't work for income.

You should prioritize working on assets that generate income.

Assets that you can sell later.

And more importantly – assets that can generate income without your direct involvement.

If your business relies on you to operate, you don't own a business.

You own a job.

If you want to do something big, you have to have a vision,

create the plan, and build systems that execute the plan.

You should only spend your time on high-leverage activities.

In the beginning, that will be marketing and sales, to validate your idea and get things moving.

But as you gain traction, you must spend your time creating systems, and finding people to operate those systems.

You must replace yourself immediately, and focus exclusively on one thing: growing your business.

Because if you're stuck in the day-to-day operations of your business, you'll never grow bigger than yourself.

But if you're creating smart systems…

The sky is the limit.

A smart system needs the following to run properly:

1. Documented Process (aka Standard Operating Procedure)
2. Schedule (how often the system gets executed)
3. Decision Making Guidelines (for your employees)
4. Ability To Measure Metrics Of The System

This paradigm shift got me to thinking about…

...how I spend my time, and how much my time is worth...

...what systems I can create in my life and business to free up more time...

...and exactly where I should focus my energy and time to maximize my income.

REMEMBER YOUR PASSION

WHEN WAS THE last time you woke up energized and excited to dive into your work for the day?

Do you feel stuck? Like you're going through the motions?

Constantly trying to figure out what your life calling is?

Here's the deal…

The idea of having a passion and life calling is a bit of a deluded fantasy.

Even for those who make a living with their passion, the big idea is your *"passion"* is still work. And not every day is rainbows and butterflies when you 'follow your passion.'

But regardless of that, we all have passions, things we're naturally fascinated with, and things that make us happy.

You don't just "find" your passion by sitting around thinking about it. You find your passion by exploring ideas, trying new things, and seeing what sticks.

But first you must understand this: your passion might not be your life's work!

But it can still be a great source of joy and fulfillment in your life. And usually, when done right, it can be a source of income.

You must first forget about the money and focus on the passion.

So how do you find your passion?

I recommend sitting down with a cup of tea, no distractions, and writing down everything on your mind.

Write about ideas, your thoughts ... just literally pour your brain onto the paper.

Do this every single day for at least a month.

Then review your writing, and you'll start to see ideas and thoughts that are recurring.

You'll want to pursue these further.

Finding your passion is about "remembering" as much as it is about finding.

If this was your last month alive, how would you spend it?

What would you hope to accomplish before you die?

What were you into as a kid?

Finding your passion is about connecting with that authentic being that lives deep down inside of you.

Before your parents told you that idea was stupid…

Before you started wearing your social mask…

And before your inner belief system told you that what you really care about isn't worth pursuing.

To find your passion, you must unpeel the layers and look deep within.

You're Perfect

THERE'S A THEME amongst most who read my work. Many seem to be too hard on themselves, and carrying around the feeling of "not being enough."

I can certainly relate.

We all feel we can do better, achieve more, and be happier. But instead of wishing for more, it's much wiser to express gratitude and set the intention to show up, be present, and focused on whatever it is we are working on improving.

The end result is not as important as how you embark upon the process.

The only thing that matters is that you are present, and your energy is used for the right reasons.

And usually that comes down to self care and love.

If you feel like:

You're not good/smart/attractive enough....

If you constantly beat yourself up, and think you could do better...

You're too hard on yourself.

Most likely, one of your parents was hard on you, strict on you, and set high standards for you. They had the best intentions: to make you the best, make you successful, make up for their own shortcomings.

But what really happens, is they instill self doubt and the feeling of "not being good enough" into your subconscious belief systems.

And it sabotages your life.

It runs your thought process and completely messes with your inner dialogue.

In this situation, there is only one thing to do.

Understand your parents had the best intentions for you, and take the best of that.

If they were hard on you, take the qualities of drive and motivation.

But leave behind the negativity. Kill the criticism and the

inner voice of your parent.

Be the loving and positive version of your parent, to yourself. You will succeed by being accepting of yourself, and compassionate with yourself.

Anytime you think "I" and "enough" in the same sentence, stop yourself and rewrite your script in a way that's more loving.

Because with every thought you think, you control your reality.

The only obstacle in life is yourself.

WHY YOU SHOULD CLIMB A MOUNTAIN

LAST WEEK, I climbed the highest free-standing mountain in the world. Physically and mentally, it was one of the hardest things I've ever done. Climbing a massive mountain is the perfect metaphor for life, overcoming obstacles, and achieving success. If you can climb a mountain like Kilimanjaro, you can do anything. Here are three life lessons I learned from the mountain:

1. Never Look Up

It's always demoralizing to see how far left you have to go. Especially when you're cold, exhausted, and mentally defeated. Most people don't ever attempt to start anything because they get paralyzed by seeing how far they have to go to get where they want. But what they don't understand is that to get there, you must:

2. Keep Your Head Down And Grind

One step at a time, one inch at a time. Just keep moving. Any action, especially imperfect action, is a thousand times better than staying in the same place, paralyzed by fear. Every step you take brings you that much closer to your goal. No matter how big or small. At around 20,000 feet up, if you stop moving, you risk freezing and getting hypothermia. And in life, when you stop moving toward your goals, toward what you believe in, you risk getting stuck exactly where you are. The longer you wait, the higher your chance of 'freezing' in the comfort zone. Which brings me to the next lesson:

3. Enjoy The Journey

The process is everything. If you can't learn to enjoy every step along the way, good and bad, you'll lose patience and give up. This game of life is a marathon, not a sprint. The mountain taught me to embrace the uncomfortable and to forego short term pleasure for long term gain. Consistency trumps everything. I landed in Tanzania knowing that success was not guaranteed. So many people made sure to tell me about their friends who "didn't make it up" for a variety of reasons. They made sure to tell me about their friends who "almost died" and to not feel bad if I don't make it to the top. The 5 day route we took had a 27% summit success rate. Multiple times during the trek I felt that I wasn't going to make it. Nothing good in life is guaranteed, but you should never let that stop you from trying. Which brings me to the last lesson:

4. Celebrate Your Wins

No matter how small or large. Every milestone matters. Celebrating reinforces the "work hard and get rewarded" system in your brain. We reinforce the idea that if we set a goal and work towards it, the outcome will be positive.

This reminds the brain what the process of achieving anything worthwhile in life looks like: Goal Setting -> Planning -> Deadline -> Commitment -> Discipline ---> Accomplishment -> Satisfaction -> Bigger Goal -> Repeat.

Climbing Kilimanjaro

THE DAY BEGAN at 6am.

We woke to brave the cold at 15,000 feet, prepare our gear, and have a quick breakfast before leaving camp. An 8 hour climb brought us to base camp, where we were served an early dinner around 5pm and quickly retired into our tents for much needed rest.

A few hours later, around 1130pm, we did a final gear inspection, had some coffee, and went off to summit Mount Kilimanjaro at 20,000 feet.

We spent the next nine hours in the dark, climbing a steep uphill with no oxygen while battling freezing winds and -20 degree weather. It was so cold, we risked hypothermia every time we tried to take a short 2-3 minute break on the way up.

The oxygen up there was so thin, you found yourself out of breath and gasping for air with every small step taken. And to top it off, our camelbacks and water supply froze, which added dehydration to our list of problems.

We arrived at the summit nine hours later at 9:15am, took a few pictures, and rapidly descended before altitude sickness could take over and potentially become deadly.

Four hours later, we arrived back at base camp, where we quickly ate and proceeded to take the best nap of our lives.

Waking up from that nap, we were still extremely exhausted, dehydrated, and suffering from symptoms of altitude sickness.

But the feeling of deep satisfaction had overtaken all of that. We had just climbed the highest free-standing mountain in the world.

Before you go, I want you to remember one thing.

You're going to die.

Sooner than you think.

My friend and colleague, Paul Gabriel Mihalescu, shared this saying with me weeks before he unexpectedly passed away.

"Memento Mori"

It's Latin and translates to 'Remember that you are going to die.'

Each day, each minute, only brings us closer to the inevitable.

Stop fucking around and wasting time.

Do that thing you want to do.

Hustle. Move forward daily.

And don't ever forget to enjoy the ride.

Because the only guarantee you've got in this life?

Is death.

If you want all the resources mentioned in this book, the bonus lessons that didn't make it into the book, and to get new lessons in your e-mail, go to AlonShabo.com/Resources

ACKNOWLEDGEMENTS

Writing a book is in many ways like climbing a mountain, and you wouldn't be reading these words if it weren't for these people....

Of course, my parents – for deciding it would be a good idea to have sex with each other.

For Neil Strauss and Rico Rivera, grateful for your mentorship, and for taking a chance on this up and coming copywriter.

For John Romaniello – a great pseudo mentor who indirectly taught me how to be a better human, writer, and entrepreneur.

For Paul Gabriel Mihalescu, my colleague and homie. You left us way too soon.

For Dana Lindahl, for opening my eyes to the transformative power of nature, and inviting me to the 'entrepreneurs trek' through the Himalayas of Nepal.

And to Freddy Lansky --- I'll never forget marching through those freak Himalayan snow-storms together.

That trip changed my life in the best way possible.

For the summit bois – Tayo Ogunnaike and Colin Specter -

Kilimanjaro was the hardest thing we've all ever done – and I'm glad we did it together.

And to Colin's soon to be wife, Robyn, for baking incredible hamentashen and gifting me the note book that birthed the big idea for this book while on Kilimanjaro.

To my lovely editor, Desiree, for staying cool when things got froggy, and handling business on a tight deadline --- this book is awesome because of you.

And lastly…

To the readers of *Richard Arthur* and everyone else who has interacted with my work – especially those that gave supportive words, and encouraged me to pursue this calling.

I wouldn't have written any of this if it weren't for you, my readers.

ABOUT THE AUTHOR

Alon Shabo is an entrepreneur, writer, and marketing consultant to the personal development industry.

His advertising promotions are responsible for millions of dollars in profits for his select clients --- many of which are household names.

For fun, he likes to climb mountains, and tries to go hiking in nature every single day.

For more, visit www.AlonShabo.com

35599947R00153

Made in the USA
San Bernardino, CA
12 May 2019